THE EVERYTHING
LARGE-PRINT CRYPTOGRAMS BOOK

Dear Reader,

Do you like solving word puzzles and cryptograms? Do you enjoy reading quotations from your favorite athletes, politicians, and entertainers? If so, you'll love this book!

I wrote *The Everything® Large-Print Cryptograms Book* as an escape from time-consuming everyday tasks. Sometimes it's fun to sit down, solve a cryptogram, and find an interesting quotation that you can ponder as you complete your day.

In this book you will find cryptograms on many different commonplace topics. Each puzzle's solution contains a quotation or maxim that relates to that chapter's topic. Some of the puzzles will be easy to solve and some of them will give you a chance to maximize your brainpower! If you do get stuck, each cryptogram has a clue at the end of each chapter to assist you.

XJIU POL (Have fun)!

Nikki Katz

Welcome to the EVERYTHING® Series!

These handy, accessible books give you all you need to tackle a difficult project, gain a new hobby, comprehend a fascinating topic, prepare for an exam, or even brush up on something you learned back in school but have since forgotten.

You can choose to read an *Everything*® book from cover to cover or just pick out the information you want from our four useful boxes: e-questions, e-facts, e-alerts, and e-ssentials. We give you everything you need to know on the subject, but throw in a lot of fun stuff along the way, too.

We now have more than 400 *Everything*® books in print, spanning such wide-ranging categories as weddings, pregnancy, cooking, music instruction, foreign language, crafts, pets, New Age, and so much more. When you're done reading them all, you can finally say you know *Everything*®!

PUBLISHER Karen Cooper

DIRECTOR OF ACQUISITIONS AND INNOVATION Paula Munier

MANAGING EDITOR, EVERYTHING® SERIES Lisa Laing

COPY CHIEF Casey Ebert

ACQUISITIONS EDITOR Lisa Laing/Hillary Thompson

EDITORIAL ASSISTANT Hillary Thompson

EVERYTHING® SERIES COVER DESIGNER Erin Alexander

LAYOUT DESIGNERS Colleen Cunningham, Elisabeth Lariviere, Ashley Vierra, Denise Wallace

Visit the entire Everything® series at *www.everything.com*

THE EVERYTHING®
LARGE-PRINT CRYPTOGRAMS BOOK

Easy-to-read, fun-to-solve puzzles

Nikki Katz

Avon, Massachusetts

To my family

An Everything® Series Book.

Everything® and everything.com® are registered trademarks of F+W Media, Inc.

Contains material adapted and abridged from *The Everything® Cryptograms Book* by Nikki Katz, copyright © 2005 by F+W Media, Inc., ISBN 10: 1-59337-319-8, ISBN 13: 978-1-59337-319-1.

Some additional information adapted from *The Everything® Crosswords and Puzzles for Quote Lovers Book* by Charles Timmerman, copyright © 2008 by F+W Media, Inc., ISBN 10: 1-59869-718-8, ISBN 13: 978-1-59869-718-6.

Published by Adams Media, a division of F+W Media, Inc.

57 Littlefield Street, Avon, MA 02322 U.S.A.

www.adamsmedia.com

ISBN 10: 1-4405-0323-0

ISBN 13: 978-1-4405-0323-8

Printed in the United States of America.

10 9 8 7 6 5 4 3 2 1

This book is available at quantity discounts for bulk purchases. For information, please call 1-800-289-0963.

Acknowledgments

Thank you to my agent, Barb Doyen at Doyen and Doyen Literary Services Inc. and to the multiple editors I worked with at Adams Media—including Kate McBride, Gina Chaimanis, and Julie Gutin.

I would also like to thank my husband, Jason, and my children—Katelyn, Kendall, and Lincoln. Their support is fundamental in allowing me to take time to write, time that is, in essence, away from them.

Contents

Introduction

ARE YOU GETTING bored with finding and solving
crossword puzzles? Still looking for someone to join
you in playing a game of hangman or Scrabble?
Or are you just looking for a new way to pass the
time on your next airplane trip or daily commute?
If you answered "yes" to any of these questions,
then *The Everything® Large-Print Cryptograms
Book* is perfect for you. Cryptograms are word
games that challenge your brain as you attempt to
solve puzzles and codes. The puzzles you'll find in
this book will also give you a chance to test your
memory of various quotations on many topics.
These cryptograms are fun for both the novice and
the expert. Some are simpler, lengthier puzzles
with more language clues to decipher, and some
puzzles are more challenging with shorter and
more obscure quotations.

Almost everyone has used codes to hide information at some point in his or her life. Perhaps as a child you wrote and deciphered secret messages by using a code you shared with your friends . . . or maybe you wrote in your journal in a code so that your parents and teachers could not understand it . . . or perhaps you talked in pig Latin to your friends in the hopes that others would not know what you were saying . . . or maybe you drew pictures that incorporated a code or various images that only the recipient would understand. But even if you did not use codes in these situations, you probably have read or spoken acronyms and abbreviations, which are actually codes as well! They are a method of shortening a longer word or phrase, but when you speak or hear them, you understand the complete meaning behind the shortened variation.

The Everything® Large-Print Cryptograms Book is a great resource for practicing your code-solving skills as it teaches you exactly what cryptograms are, provides tips for solving them, and offers multiple chapters of cryptogram puzzles to practice your skills with plenty of room to work. If you get stuck on any particular puzzle, make sure to check the end of each chapter for a hint word.

Please note that as you are solving the puzzles you may find that a coded letter (or two) in a particular puzzle is the same as the uncoded letter within the solution. This is not an attempt to trick you or throw you off. It is just the nature of cryptograms! There is no specific way to convert the letters, so often one letter's conversion will be itself.

Now you are ready to start enjoying this book. Head to Chapter 1 if you are new to cryptograms or need a quick refresher, or skip to any of the other chapters to start solving puzzles in a topic of interest to you!

Cryptograms 101

Cryptograms are fun word puzzles consisting of phrases and text that have been converted into code. When you solve a cryptogram, you won't get the solution to the code. You'll have to figure it out yourself based on your knowledge of the English language. This chapter provides basic terminology to get you started, a quick history of cryptograms, general tips for solving the puzzles, and an example solution.

BASIC TERMINOLOGY

There are many different terms used in the cryptographic language. To start with, the message to be coded is written originally in plaintext or cleartext. The act of encoding that message to hide the contents from another reader is called encryption. The message after it has been encrypted is in a cryptogram or ciphertext. The act of decoding the message and turning the ciphertext back into plaintext is called decryption. The key, if available, shows the code and is used to decrypt the ciphertext.

The science of cryptograms is called cryptography and the people who study it are called cryptographers. The act of breaking a cipher, without knowing the key, is called cryptanalysis and the people who perform cryptanalysis are called cryptanalysts.

A cipher is a cryptographic system or method of encryption and decryption. In a transposition cipher, the letters in the original plaintext are rearranged within the original message. The message could be written backwards, each word could be written backwards, or the letters could be scrambled. A substitution cipher is one in which each letter of the plaintext is replaced with another letter or symbol. In a simple substitution each letter of the plaintext is always replaced with the same letter or symbol. No other letters use that symbol. There is a one-to-one relationship in the key. In a polyalphabetic substitution cipher, two or more cipher alphabets are used to make the encryption more secure.

HISTORY OF CRYPTOLOGY

The history of cryptology dates back to approximately 1900 B.C. It was discovered that an Egyptian scribe used nonstandard hieroglyphics in his communication. Over time, cryptology was used in other parts of the world. For instance, around 1500 B.C., a Mesopotamian tablet recorded an encrypted recipe for making pottery glazes. In approximately 500 B.C., Hebrew scribes used the Atbash Cipher to write the book of Jeremiah. Around 400 B.C., Spartans used a "scytale" cipher device to communicate between military commanders. In 50–60 B.C., the Caesar Cipher was created by Julius Caesar to communicate with his army.

As civilization moved forward, so did the use and understanding of cryptology. The Arabs used both substitution and transposition ciphers, and by approximately A.D. 1412 al-Kalka-shandi included several cryptographic systems in his encyclopedia. Europeans began using cryptography in the Middle Ages, often substituting only the vowels within their plaintext. A cryptography manual was published around 1379 by Gabriele de Lavinde of Parma, who served Pope Clement VII. The Rosetta Stone, found in Egypt in 1799, was encrypted with the same message in Greek and Egyptian, and in hieroglyphics.

During the last few centuries, cryptograms became very useful to cloak communications during times of war. In the American Civil War, the Federal army used transposition ciphers for their communication. The Confederate army used the Vigenere Cipher, which the Union army could typically solve. In World War I and World War II, all military operations were using cryptography. The German army used the Enigma machine to create supposedly unbreakable codes for their radio messages. Fortunately, they were actually breakable and this helped the Allies to win the war.

The field of cryptography remained well hidden until computers became more popular and more affordable to the general public. As digital communication increased, the demand for encryption grew. In 1977, the National Bureau of Standards published the Data Encryption Standard (DES) for use by governmental agencies and banks. That same year, Ron Rivest, Adi Shamir, and Leonard Adleman developed RSA, an Internet encryption and authentication algorithm. It is included in the Netscape and Internet Explorer browsers.

FAMOUS CIPHERS

There are quite a few well-known historical ciphers that are still being used to code simple messages. These codes include the Vigenere Cipher, the Caesar Cipher, and the Atbash Cipher, all of which are described in detail below.

Vigenere Cipher

The Vigenere Cipher was created by Blaise de Vigenere, a member of the court of Henry III of France during the sixteenth century. This cipher is a polyalphabetic substitution cipher requiring the following table and a keyword, where the keyword is a random word that is used to help encrypt the message.

Vigenere Cipher

	A	**B**	**C**	**D**	**E**	**F**	**G**	**H**	**I**	**J**	**K**	**L**
A:	A	B	C	D	E	F	G	H	I	J	K	L
B:	B	C	D	E	F	G	H	I	J	K	L	M
C:	C	D	E	F	G	H	I	J	K	L	M	N
D:	D	E	F	G	H	I	J	K	L	M	N	O
E:	E	F	G	H	I	J	K	L	M	N	O	P
F:	F	G	H	I	J	K	L	M	N	O	P	Q
G:	G	H	I	J	K	L	M	N	O	P	Q	R
H:	H	I	J	K	L	M	N	O	P	Q	R	S
I:	I	J	K	L	M	N	O	P	Q	R	S	T
J:	J	K	L	M	N	O	P	Q	R	S	T	U
K:	K	L	M	N	O	P	Q	R	S	T	U	V
L:	L	M	N	O	P	Q	R	S	T	U	V	W
M:	M	N	O	P	Q	R	S	T	U	V	W	X

M	**N**	**O**	**P**	**Q**	**R**	**S**	**T**	**U**	**V**	**W**	**X**	**Y**	**Z**
M	N	O	P	Q	R	S	T	U	V	W	X	Y	Z
N	O	P	Q	R	S	T	U	V	W	X	Y	Z	A
O	P	Q	R	S	T	U	V	W	X	Y	Z	A	B
P	Q	R	S	T	U	V	W	X	Y	Z	A	B	C
Q	R	S	T	U	V	W	X	Y	Z	A	B	C	D
R	S	T	U	V	W	X	Y	Z	A	B	C	D	E
S	T	U	V	W	X	Y	Z	A	B	C	D	E	F
T	U	V	W	X	Y	Z	A	B	C	D	E	F	G
U	V	W	X	Y	Z	A	B	C	D	E	F	G	H
V	W	X	Y	Z	A	B	C	D	E	F	G	H	I
W	X	Y	Z	A	B	C	D	E	F	G	H	I	J
X	Y	Z	A	B	C	D	E	F	G	H	I	J	K
Y	Z	A	B	C	D	E	F	G	H	I	J	K	L

Vigenere Cipher (continued)

N:	N	O	P	Q	R	S	T	U	V	W	X	Y
O:	O	P	Q	R	S	T	U	V	W	X	Y	Z
P:	P	Q	R	S	T	U	V	W	X	Y	Z	A
Q:	Q	R	S	T	U	V	W	X	Y	Z	A	B
R:	R	S	T	U	V	W	X	Y	Z	A	B	C
S:	S	T	U	V	W	X	Y	Z	A	B	C	D
T:	T	U	V	W	X	Y	Z	A	B	C	D	E
U:	U	V	W	X	Y	Z	A	B	C	D	E	F
V:	V	W	X	Y	Z	A	B	C	D	E	F	G
W:	W	X	Y	Z	A	B	C	D	E	F	G	H
X:	X	Y	Z	A	B	C	D	E	F	G	H	I
Y:	Y	Z	A	B	C	D	E	F	G	H	I	J
Z:	Z	A	B	C	D	E	F	G	H	I	J	K

```
Z  A  B  C  D  E  F  G  H  I  J  K  L  M
A  B  C  D  E  F  G  H  I  J  K  L  M  N
B  C  D  E  F  G  H  I  J  K  L  M  N  O
C  D  E  F  G  H  I  J  K  L  M  N  O  P
D  E  F  G  H  I  J  K  L  M  N  O  P  Q
E  F  G  H  I  J  K  L  M  N  O  P  Q  R
F  G  H  I  J  K  L  M  N  O  P  Q  R  S
G  H  I  J  K  L  M  N  O  P  Q  R  S  T
H  I  J  K  L  M  N  O  P  Q  R  S  T  U
I  J  K  L  M  N  O  P  Q  R  S  T  U  V
J  K  L  M  N  O  P  Q  R  S  T  U  V  W
K  L  M  N  O  P  Q  R  S  T  U  V  W  X
L  M  N  O  P  Q  R  S  T  U  V  W  X  Y
```

Let's say you wished to encrypt the phrase LOVE ALL, TRUST A FEW, DO WRONG TO NONE using the keyword TURNIP. You would start off by writing the word TURNIP above the phrase as many times as it takes to complete it. Then to determine the ciphertext, use the letter at the intersection of the row using the keyword letter and the column using the phrase letter.

Vigenere Cipher Example

T	U	R	N	I	P	T	U	R	N	I	P	T	U	R	N
L	O	V	E	A	L	L	T	R	U	S	T	A	F	E	W
E	I	M	R	I	A	E	N	I	H	A	I	T	Z	V	J

I	P	T	U	R	N	I	P	T	U	R	N	I
D	O	W	R	O	N	G	T	O	N	O	N	E
L	D	P	L	F	A	O	I	H	H	F	A	M

If given the ciphertext, you would need the keyword to decrypt the message. You would write the keyword multiple times over the ciphertext and then use the row of the keyword letter, follow along the row until you found the ciphertext letter, and follow that up the column to find the corresponding plaintext solution.

Caesar Cipher

It is very simple to encrypt and decrypt messages using the Caesar Cipher. The plaintext letters are replaced by ciphertext letters that are three places down the alphabet: The letter A is replaced with the letter D, the letter B is replaced with the letter E, and so on.

Caesar Cipher

A	B	C	D	E	F	G	H	I	J	K	L	M
D	E	F	G	H	I	J	K	L	M	N	O	P
N	**O**	**P**	**Q**	**R**	**S**	**T**	**U**	**V**	**W**	**X**	**Y**	**Z**
Q	R	S	T	U	V	W	X	Y	Z	A	B	C

Atbash Cipher

The Atbash Cipher is another simple substitution code. It is one of the few ciphers to use the Hebrew language. The Hebrew word *atbash* actually tells us the substitution method used. The first letter, *aleph*, is followed by the last letter, *tav*. The second letter, *beth*, is followed by the second to last letter, *shin*. In using the Atbash Cipher for the English language, A is replaced by Z, B is replaced by Y, and so on.

Atbash Cipher

A	B	C	D	E	F	G	H	I	J	K	L	M
Z	Y	X	W	V	U	T	S	R	Q	P	O	N

N	O	P	Q	R	S	T	U	V	W	X	Y	Z
M	L	K	J	I	H	G	F	E	D	C	B	A

UNSOLVED CRYPTOGRAMS

Not all cryptograms are easy to solve. In fact, there are many famous unsolved codes and ciphers. The Voynich manuscript, which is over 400 years old, is a nearly 235-page manuscript that is written entirely in a strange, unknown alphabet.

Another unsolved cipher was one sent on July 14, 1897, by composer Edward Elgar. He sent a letter to a friend, Dora Penny, written completely in code. She was unable to read the letter, and he never explained it. Miss Penny attempted to have other people solve it, but to this day the code has not been cracked.

In another example of an unsolved code, archaeologist Sir Arthur Evans uncovered clay tablets with mysterious symbols in Crete in 1900. He spent a great amount of time attempting to decrypt the three different writing systems used (a hieroglyphic script, and two systems later referred to as Linear A and Linear B). To this day, only Linear B has been solved.

In the late 1960s, a serial killer, nicknamed the Zodiac Killer, sent multiple coded communications to the police and editors of publications. Some of those letters were solved, but many were not.

The Edgar Allan Poe Cryptographic Challenge is a famous cryptogram that was just recently solved. Poe was enthralled with cryptography and challenged his readers to send him cryptograms to solve. A "Mr. W. B. Tyler" submitted two cryptograms to Poe and Poe never found solutions for them. Instead he challenged his audience to solve them. It was speculated that perhaps Poe created the cryptograms himself, but nobody has been able to prove it. Gil Broza of Toronto cracked the cipher 150 years later.

TIPS FOR SOLVING CRYPTOGRAMS

Now that you know what a cryptogram is, it's time for some tips to help you solve the puzzles you'll find here. In this book the cryptograms use simple substitutions to encrypt interesting quotations. Each letter of the quotation will be replaced by a different letter, but the original spacing and punctuation is retained. Since you will not be given the key, your job is to decipher the puzzle using the topic given and your knowledge of the English language.

Common Letters and Words

In English, E is the most common letter, followed by T, A, O, N, I, and R. The words A and I are the most common one-letter words, with O coming in at a very distant third place. The most common two-letter words are OF, TO, IN, IS, IT, BE, BY, HE, AS, ON, AT, OR, AN, SO, IF, and NO. The most common three-letter words are THE and AND, followed by FOR, HIS, NOT, BUT, YOU, ARE, HER, and HAD. The most common four-letter word is THAT, followed by WITH, HAVE, and FROM. If you see a four-letter word that begins and ends in the same letter, you might want to try THAT first.

The letter Q is always followed by U. The letter E is the most common letter at the end of a word, and T is the most common letter at the beginning of a word. If there is an apostrophe in the puzzle, it means that the word is either possessive (John's) or a contraction (won't). If a single letter follows the apostrophe, it's usually an S or a T. If the letter is a T, the letter before the apostrophe is an N.

Don't Forget the Vowels

When it comes to vowels, the majority of two-letter words start with an A, I, O, or U and end with an E, O, or Y. The letters O and E are often seen in double letters, whereas the other vowels are rarely seen as doubles. The letter A is usually seen as the initial letter in a word or the second letter from the end. The letter E is usually seen as the second letter in a word or the final letter, but is also scattered throughout words. The letter I is most often seen as the third letter from the end (ION and ING being common endings). The letter O is usually seen as the second letter in a word or the final letter. The letter U is typically seen as the first letter in a word or the second letter from the end. The letter Y is usually the last letter in a word.

Where Do I Start?

Solving cryptograms involves a lot of trial and error. You may want to start out by counting the letters and guessing that the most common letter is an E. Although this often gives you a good jump-start, there may be a few puzzles that have no E's at all. Knowing one or two letters of a word can often help you solve the rest of the word and gives you letters in other words within the puzzle. Words that commonly go together, like IT IS, can be helpful as well. Longer cryptograms are easier to solve than shorter ones because they offer more instances of letters and patterns.

FOR EXAMPLE

Now that you've seen some tips for solving cryptograms, here is an example and the corresponding solution. You'll be solving the following cryptogram:

GQP XBHHPEPDFP APGIPPD GQP EBTQG INEX KDX GQP KCUNJG EBTQG INEX BJ GQP XBHHPEPDFP APGIPPD CBTQGDBDT KDX K CBTQGDBDT AVT.

—UKEZ GIKBD

A good first step is to count the letters and see which occurs most often. In this case, it's the letter P, which probably means that it represents the letter E.

Letter Count

A	B	C	D	E	F	G	H	I	J	K	L	M	N
3	10	3	11	7	2	12	4	5	2	6	0	0	3

O	P	Q	R	S	T	U	V	W	X	Y	Z
0	16	8	0	0	7	2	1	0	6	0	1

If you look for the most common three-letter word in the puzzle you will see that GQP occurs four times. That combination is most likely the word THE. Since you've already speculated that P is E, your guess is probably correct. Therefore you can now go into the puzzle and substitute E for P, T for G, and H for Q.

The puzzle now looks like this (note that decoded letters are indicated by lower case):

the XBHHeEeDFe AetleeD the EBTht INEX KDX the KCUNJt EBTht INEX BJ the XBHHeEeDFe AetleeD CBThtDBDT KDX K CBThtDBDT AVT.

—UKEZ tIKBD

If you now look at the second most common three-letter word, you will see that KDX occurs two times. You'll also see that

K appears as a single letter one time. This probably signifies that K is A and KDX is AND. Therefore you can substitute A for K, N for D, and D for X, which gives the following:

the dBHHeEenFe Aetleen the EBTht INEd and the aCUNJt EBTht INEd BJ the dBHHeEenFe Aetleen CBThtnBnT and a CBThtnBnT AVT.

—UaEZ tlaBn

Looking at Aetleen, you can speculate that the word is BETWEEN, so A becomes B and I becomes W. We now have:

the dBHHeEenFe between the EBTht wNEd and the aCUNJt EBTht wNEd BJ the dBHHeEenFe between CBThtnBnT and a CBThtnBnT bVT.

—UaEZ twaBn

Now looking at dBHHeEenFe and the context of the sentence, you can determine that the word is DIFFERENCE, so B becomes I, H becomes F, E becomes R, and F becomes C, which gives us:

the difference between the riTht wNrd and the aCUNJt riTht wNrd iJ the difference between CiThtninT and a CiThtninT bVT.

—UarZ twaIn

If you look at the word CiThtninT, you can speculate that the T would need to be a G, making the word Cightning, and the C would become an L for LIGHTNING. The puzzle now looks like this:

the difference between the right wNrd and the alU-NJt right wNrd iJ the difference between lightning and a lightning bVg.

—UarZ twain

When you look at iJ, you know it has to be either IT, IS, or IN. Since T and N are already accounted for, the word must be IS and the letter S can be substituted for any J's:

the dIfference between the right wNrd and the alU-Nst right wNrd is the difference between lightning and a lightning bVg.

—UarZ twain

If you look at words bVg and wNrd, you see that V and N need to be vowels. The only two vowels left are O and U, so the V is a U for BUG and the N is an O for WORD:

the difference between the right word and the alUost right word is the difference between lightning and a lightning bug.

—UarZ twain

Now, it's easy to see that alUost is "almost," so the U is an M. If you look at the author of the quotation you can probably guess that it is Mark Twain, so the Z becomes a K. The solved puzzle is:

The difference between the right word and the almost right word is the difference between lightning and a lightning bug.

—Mark Twain

Example Cryptogram: Reference Code

A	B	C	D	E	F	G	H	I	J	K	L	M	N
K	A	F	X	P	H	T	Q	B	R	Z	C	U	D

O	P	Q	R	S	T	U	V	W	X	Y	Z
N	Y	L	E	J	G	V	O	I	S	M	W

CHAPTER 2

Beauty and Fashion

Beauty is in the eye of the beholder . . . which is lucky for designers! Beauty and fashion go hand in hand. The fashion world revolves around the creations of the designers, the look and display of the models, and the artwork and advertisements created by the photographers. The cryptograms in this chapter give you an inside look into the fashion industry and its top personalities.

BEAUTY AROUND US

Puzzle 2-1

X BGWER OK FCXUBP WM X NOP KOTCVCT; WBM YOVCYWECMM WEJTCXMCM; WB DWYY ECVCT IXMM WEBO EOBGWERECMM.

—NOGE HCXBM

_____

_____

_____

_____

Puzzle 2-2

PH CTCVN EWH'G SCWVR RSCVC PG W GCXVCR HCVTC RSWR WHGDCVG RA RSC TPIVWRPAHG AU ICWMRN.

—XSVPGRAFSCV EAVOCN

_____

_____

_____

_____

answers on page 248

Puzzle 2-3

WVBOTI FH AMV AS TZV KBKV TZFMDH TZBT
NA MAT CVBN TA NAOWT AS DAN.

—UVBM BMAOFCZ

_____

_____

_____

_____

Puzzle 2-4

QOX PIKXHB KXI AXONS WMHP K TIKOHY QOX
IYIB VQOZA NIRIX BII.

—DIQXDI W. XOBBIZZ

_____

_____

_____

_____

answers on page 248

Puzzle 2-5

KJQ HQWEKU KJWK WOOAQNNQN PKNQLD
KG KJQ QUQN PN GFLU KJQ NMQLL GD KJQ
BGBQFK; KJQ QUQ GD KJQ HGOU PN FGK
WLTWUN KJWK GD KJQ NGEL.

—CQGACQ NWFO

answer on page 248

Puzzle 2-6

NTXPMD GTJVKCTG UL KMB JVUJTV LUKAB
XZG XGSPZYMB YTXBTB MU NT TZSUDTG
XB NTXPMD, SPBM XB AKIQM GTJVKCTG UL
XAA BQXGUWB YTXBTB MU NT TZSUDTG XB
AKIQM.

—SUQZ VPBRKZ

_____

_____

_____

_____

_____

_____

_____

_____

_____

_____

answer on page 248

FASHION ADVICE

Puzzle 2-7

TNQNQSNT GCRG RXMRDJ LTNJJEAP EA
ZALNTJGRGNL PHHL GRJGN EJ GCN JRQN RJ
VXRDEAP LNRL.

—JZJRA IRGCNTEAN

_____

_____

_____

_____

Puzzle 2-8

T MYSTO'C AZWCC CDYGFA EW FHIW T ETZEWA-
MHZW KWOVW: CWZQHOP HUC NGZNYCW
MHUDYGU YECUZGVUHOP UDW QHWM.

—CYNDHT FYZWO

_____

_____

_____

_____

answers on page 248

Puzzle 2-9

UWIPP PYDFVM. YA MEK CIXW X UYGGIW BXLRIN, UEG'N CIXW XGMNSYGQ IVPI EG YN . . . VYRI VKGLS EW UYGGIW.

—QIEWQI TKWGP

_____
_____
_____
_____

Puzzle 2-10

LGT EMTAA RNAL SBZZBO LGT VBEY BS P OBRPX, XBL LGT VBEY SBZZBOIXH LGT AGPKT BS LGT EMTAA.

—GNVTML ET HIUTXWGY

_____
_____
_____
_____

answers on page 248

Puzzle 2-11

JN QNG GDNPVRA MNPDSARK WPFH GN UAG
QAX GHZQUS, XHAGHAD FRNGHAS ND KDZAQJS
. . . . SARR MNPD FRNGHAS LQJ IAAT MNPD
GHNPUHGS.

—HAQDM JLYZJ GHNDALP

---

answer on page 249

A FASHION STATEMENT

Puzzle 2-12

RU RG FIH BVFMD YVUKIY UKVF UVGUI HKRMK
QYACWMIG GA EVFD FIH BVGKRAFG.

—JANUVRYI

_____

_____

_____

_____

Puzzle 2-13

BUFQ MYQWRUI HYEEFX? YDVYKQ — EWUPTW
IUE ZPREF YQ HPGW YMEFX BFYEW.

—CUYI XRJFXQ

_____

_____

_____

answers on page 249

Puzzle 2-14

J OKUB QD PYBR YG MTYRLKP RY PUHK QK
RLK RBYVATK YG SKMJSJXZ OLJML MTYRLKP
RY OKUB.

—IURLUBJXK LKWAVBX
_____
_____
_____
_____

Puzzle 2-15

HXQODYT DQ QYNWZODTV ZOXZ VYWQ DT
YTW AWXM XTJ YSZ YZOW YZOWM.

—JWTDQW IRXOT
_____
_____
_____
_____

answers on page 249

Puzzle 2-16

BDHIGPA GH FRACGQGCZ OUAAGAF DEDZ
BOPX YUQFDOGCZ, DAS DBODGS PB VRGAF
PYROCDWRA VZ GC. GC GH D HGFA CIR CEP
CIGAFH DOR APC BDO DHUASRO.

—EGQQGDX IDMQGCC

_____

_____

_____

_____

_____

_____

_____

_____

_____

_____

answer on page 249

Puzzle 2-17

VX VGAKZT DCODOAZR AKYA D KYR AG ATX
AKDCPO GC AG VYWZ OFTZ AKZX QZTZ
UZBGVDCP. UZBGVDCP QKYA, D YEQYXO
YOWZR.

—ZRDAK WGCZBWX

_____

_____

_____

_____

_____

_____

_____

_____

_____

_____

_____

answer on page 249

Puzzle 2-18

JXTHZC   ES   SXCGHEA   CFXLYZ   FGZHL
GXVVHAZCC FE SZZT FGZHL YXAHFU, XAT
FGZHL JEYZ FE SZZT FGZHL VLHTZ.
                    —QGXLJZC QXJZD QEJFEA

_____

_____

_____

_____

_____

_____

_____

_____

_____

_____

answer on page 249

TOP DESIGNERS

Puzzle 2-19

KYMI JAUER MJ AKR PMXYE AMC-SPP NKRAKRI
SI XSA Y NSOYX IRYEEU VXSNJ KRIJREP.

—KLWRIA BR DMZRXTKU

_____

_____

_____

_____

Puzzle 2-20

I DFPCVAFU CP KAMG IP VKKD IP BZF PBIU TZK
TFIUP ZFU EMKBZFP.

—FDCBZ ZFID

_____

_____

_____

_____

answers on page 249

Puzzle 2-21

B XBON B NMJ BLGTLYTJ ZVST ITMLO. YNTH NMGT TCQETOOBAL, RAJTOYH, OTC MQQTMV, OBRQVBPBYH — MVV B NAQT FAE BL RH PVAYNTO.

—HGTO OMBLY VMSETLY

_____

_____

_____

_____

_____

_____

_____

_____

_____

_____

answer on page 249

Puzzle 2-22

LTYDAKG TGFAOAMTFPY, TGB PQPWTGOP AY T
YFTFP KL HAGB . . . T HAVVKV KL FDP FAHP
AG UDAOD UP QAZP, T FVTGYQTFAKG KL FDP
LSFSVP, TGB YDKSQB GPZPV JP YFTFAO.

—KQPW OTYYAGA

_____

_____

_____

_____

_____

_____

_____

_____

_____

_____

_____

answer on page 250

Puzzle 2-23

FG BZUECZPP . . . KP USVNKXZVXLSZ. K XNKCE
AW FG BASE UP ZONZFZSUR USVNKXZVXLSZ,
DZDKVUXZD XA XNZ HZULXG AW XNZ WZFURZ
HADG.

—VNSKPXKUC DKAS

_____

_____

_____

_____

_____

_____

_____

_____

_____

_____

_____

_____

answer on page 250

MIND OVER MODEL

Puzzle 2-24

MXVZD XA XQT KEMVZM, QAFC AS XA HAGO
JENVFH ESC JOVTSCM—XQTH UVFF STPTO BA
AGX AJ JEMQVAS.

—SVDV XEHFAO

_____

_____

_____

_____

Puzzle 2-25

WP FXZ BFJAWN, W AN FGH FN XCEZ C FXNJMXF
WP LH XZCA, BN FXCF WF'B PNF RWOZ C URCPO
BFCGZ.

—KWPAH KGCVSNGA

_____

_____

_____

_____

answers on page 250

Puzzle 2-26

HS TPCQDHSW, LGQNQ HX SP FPHSL HS LNBHSW LP FNPMQ BPR GUMQ U VNUHS, XP JGB QMQS VPLGQN? H'C XPPSQN XUMQ LGQ QSQNWB KPN XPTQLGHSW TPNQ TQUSHSWKRD.

—GQDQSU ZGNHXLQSXQS

_____

_____

_____

_____

_____

_____

_____

_____

_____

_____

_____

answer on page 250

Puzzle 2-27

K MDKYG QEAM ULEUBL CIL RVIKEVA CZEVM
PDCM KM PEVBT ZL BKGL ME ZL CZBL ME QLLM
SEVIALBN — KM'A LLIKL.

     —RDIKAMS MVIBKYHMEY

answer on page 250

Puzzle 2-28

LMHK UKMUDK CJYK JTVAYK AHJWAPJVAMPL,
OIV VCKB GMP'V ZPMQ HK JPG VCKB'SK QSMPW
AE VCKB VCAPZ VCKB GM.

—BJHADJ GAJR

_____

_____

_____

_____

_____

_____

_____

_____

_____

answer on page 250

HINTS

Puzzle 2-1: The word "never" is found in this puzzle.

Puzzle 2-2: The word "heart" is found in this puzzle.

Puzzle 2-3: The word "rare" is found in this puzzle.

Puzzle 2-4: The word "drunk" is found in this puzzle.

Puzzle 2-5: The word "beauty" is found in this puzzle.

Puzzle 2-6: The word "ceases" is found in this puzzle.

Puzzle 2-7: The word "taste" is found in this puzzle.

Puzzle 2-8: The word "dress" is found in this puzzle.

Puzzle 2-9: The word "lunch" is found in this puzzle.

Puzzle 2-10: The word "shape" is found in this puzzle.

Puzzle 2-11: The word "trouble" is found in this puzzle.

Puzzle 2-12: The word "fancy" is found in this puzzle.

Puzzle 2-13: The word "quite" is found in this puzzle.

Puzzle 2-14: The word "sort" is found in this puzzle.

Puzzle 2-15: The word "goes" is found in this puzzle.

Puzzle 2-16: The word "afraid" is found in this puzzle.

Puzzle 2-17: The word "mother" is found in this puzzle.

Puzzle 2-18: The word "pride" is found in this puzzle.

Puzzle 2-19: The word "knows" is found in this puzzle.

Puzzle 2-20: The word "only" is found in this puzzle.

Puzzle 2-21: The word "blue" is found in this puzzle.

Puzzle 2-22: The word "should" is found in this puzzle.

Puzzle 2-23: The word "female" is found in this puzzle.

Puzzle 2-24: The word "family" is found in this puzzle.

Puzzle 2-25: The word "stare" is found in this puzzle.

Puzzle 2-26: The word "energy" is found in this puzzle.

Puzzle 2-27: The word "would" is found in this puzzle.

Puzzle 2-28: The word "wrong" is found in this puzzle.

CHAPTER 3

Holiday Celebrations

What is a holiday without some traditional songs, remarkable quotations, funny sayings, and serious expressions? You know Christmas just wouldn't be Christmas without some caroling! So take a short holiday, or just a little break in the day, and solve these cryptograms with solutions involving birthdays, Christmas, Thanksgiving, New Year's, and Halloween. Some of the quotations are fun and silly, while others are more serious and leave you with something to ponder.

HAPPY BIRTHDAY

Puzzle 3-1

O JNSEWVOZ ND XLDE EWF GNSDE VOZ PG
OYPEWFS 365-VOZ XPLSYFZ OSPLYV EWF DLY.
FYXPZ EWF ESNT!

—OLEWPS LYMYPHY

_____

_____

_____

_____

Puzzle 3-2

MRY KDLD QRLU NU RLWSWUNZ. FRU'O FWD N
JRIM.

—XRHU GNCRU

_____

_____

_____

_____

answers on page 250

Puzzle 3-3

CJV XYJB CJV KAO POHHMYP JRE BQOY HQO
IKYEROD IJDH GJAO HQKY HQO IKXO.

—LJL QJWO

_____

_____

_____

_____

Puzzle 3-4

ISMN PCQCQUCP, BHEC TBS'PC BYCP NKC KJVV
TBS UCDJH NB ZJEF SZ MZCCX.

—EKWPVCM MEKSVNO

_____

_____

_____

_____

answers on pages 250–251

Puzzle 3-5

CMAUA RUA CMUAA MDHOUAO RHO FBXCT-PYDU ORTF VMAH TYD JBIMC IAC DH-ZBUCMORT KUAFAHCF. . .RHO YHNT YHA PYU ZBUCMORT KUAFAHCF, TYD LHYV.

—NAVBF SRUUYNN

_____

_____

_____

_____

_____

_____

_____

_____

_____

_____

_____

answer on page 251

Puzzle 3-6

VB NQXUAIRB! JARU R IQOODXDYU CLHYI
UARU JLXI ARI QY VB BLHUAOHE DRXC;
RYI ALJ DRTA UQVD UAD IRB TLVDC XLHYI,
EDCC RYI EDCC JAQUD QUC VRXG RZZDRXC.
　　　　　　　　　　　　—UALVRC VLLXD

_____

_____

_____

_____

_____

_____

_____

_____

_____

_____

_____

_____

answer on page 251

MERRY CHRISTMAS

Puzzle 3-7

CIYLEOJHE XHMWE H JHFLC XHDN TMWY
OILE XTYBN, HDN QWITBN, WMWYUOILDF LE
ETGOWY HDN JTYW QWHPOLGPB.

       —DTYJHD MLDCWDO SWHBW

_____

_____

_____

_____

Puzzle 3-8

GFCZYPAWY, GFZORCXS, ZY SNP W RWPX. ZP
ZY W YPWPX NI AZSR.

       —AWCT XOOXS GFWYX

_____

_____

_____

_____

answers on page 251

Puzzle 3-9

PDAT BATX ZA BATX, ECW BXEDZ ZA BXEDZ, PDAT ACX FREMX ZA ECAZBXD. ZBX OEDTZB ECW KAU AP MBDVQZTEQ GDVCYQ HQ MRAQXD ZA XEMB AZBXD.

—XTVRU TEZZBXOQ

_____

_____

_____

_____

_____

_____

_____

_____

_____

_____

answer on page 251

Puzzle 3-10

QPJ HBBSX UJHJ AJHL XQIOO UPIOJ QPJ
FTVJX UJHJ XBMQOL QGHZJK TZK QPJ UIZQJH
XGZXPIZJ RHJFQ IZ QB QBGRP QPJ EHIVPQ
PJTKX TZK XJHIBGX MTRJX UIQP T RPHIXQSTX
VHJJQIZV.

—OBGIXT STL TORBQQ

_____

_____

_____

_____

_____

_____

_____

_____

_____

_____

_____

answer on page 251

CHRISTMAS CAROLS

Puzzle 3-11

L'H XPMVHLQG YU V NDLIM CDPLAIHVA,
WZAI BLJM IDM YQMA L ZAMX IY JQYN.

_____
_____
_____
_____

Puzzle 3-12

ZOBH IUO UYLLT VDIU MPWXUT PA UPLLQ
AY LY LY LY LY LY LY LY LY

_____
_____
_____
_____

answers on page 251

Puzzle 3-13

UF UYSH JDM B IFCCJ NHCYSAIBS,
BZX B HBGGJ ZFU JFBC.

_____

_____

_____

_____

Puzzle 3-14

X VXCY, BTT IY ZBWOKZRT, FXIZRT BSN
ODWRCQKBSO,
XK VXCY IY, X VXCY IY OX JYOKTYKYC.

_____

_____

_____

_____

answers on page 252

Puzzle 3-15

CMGZSV SMTUV! UWGL SMTUV!
NGG MC HNGX, NGG MC AQMTUV
QWKSR LWS YMQTMS XWVUZQ NSR HUMGR,
UWGL MSENSV CW VZSRZQ NSR XMGR,
CGZZP MS UZNYZSGL PZNHZ!

_____

_____

_____

_____

_____

_____

_____

_____

_____

_____

_____

answer on page 252

Puzzle 3-16

XZGN QCMLKNBO Z TNLLQ BWFFBN
AXLWKFTZK.
BNF QCML XNZLF VN BWDXF,
OLCT UCI CU CML FLCMVBNK
IWBB VN CMF CO KWDXF.

_____

_____

_____

_____

_____

_____

_____

_____

_____

_____

_____

answer on page 252

TRICK OR TREAT

Puzzle 3-17

U AYUTDNXPCMY EYMPMTDB BCM DXMBT'P
KTXG GCX WXS UYM XT CUZZXGMMT.

—MYNU FXNFMJK

_____

_____

_____

_____

Puzzle 3-18

MH WLOAH SRSB-SORT HIE PIRAHA FUAH PR
JMSB HR HIELO QULEH POMKEA JEDRT.

—HIERCRALM PMOOLARN

_____

_____

_____

_____

answers on page 252

Puzzle 3-19

MKXUX CH YEMKCYT NRYYJ BQERM KBGGEAXXY. MKCH HBUSBHMCS NXHMCZBG UXNGXSMH, UBMKXU, BY CYNXUYBG WXOBYW NEU UXZXYTX QJ SKCGWUXY EY MKX BWRGM AEUGW.

—VXBY QBRWUCGGBUW

_____

_____

_____

_____

_____

_____

_____

_____

_____

_____

answer on page 252

Puzzle 3-20

BTFV! BTFV IH IBA JELQ! 'IEC IBA LEPBI, IBAR CTR,

JBAL TXX CHKXC OHGA NTOV YFHG IBA YTF TJTR —

IBA QATQ, YHFPHIIAL IBEC GTLR T QTR!

—WEFLT CBATFQ

_____

_____

_____

_____

_____

_____

_____

_____

_____

_____

answer on page 252

HAPPY NEW YEAR

Puzzle 3-21

W GQX FQWT'K TQKRUAEIRG IK KRZQEDIGS EDWE SRQK IG RGQ FQWT WGL RAE EDQ REDQT.

—WAEDRT AGNGRXG

_____

_____

_____

_____

Puzzle 3-22

ARS ZJCSGA ZE F LSM ISFX UY LZA ARFA MS YRZHPV RFKS F LSM ISFX. UA UY ARFA MS YRZHPV RFKS F LSM YZHP.

—Q. W. GRSYASXAZL

_____

_____

_____

answers on page 252

Puzzle 3-23

DL TYCJFJNC NCDBN WY WLCJV FJMLJKAC CT
NZZ CAZ LZE BZDP JL. D YZNNJFJNC NCDBN
WY CT FDXZ NWPZ CAZ TVM BZDP VZDUZN.

—RJVV UDWKADL

_____

_____

_____

_____

_____

_____

_____

_____

_____

_____

_____

answer on page 253

Puzzle 3-24

SU USW WZWY YWCBYVWV IPW NXYQI UN
JBSGBYF EXIP XSVXNNWYWSLW. XI XQ IPBI
NYUT EPXLP BAA VBIW IPWXY IXTW, BSV LUGSI
GMUS EPBI XQ AWNI.

—LPBYAWQ ABTO

_____

_____

_____

_____

_____

_____

_____

_____

_____

_____

answer on page 253

GIVING THANKS

Puzzle 3-25

ZOBP   BP   ZOU   RBLUPZ   AUNPVXU   IR
ZONLHPSBCBLS: N   ZONLHRVQLUPP   ZONZ
PFXBLSP RXIA QICU.

—KBQQBNA W. PHUNZO

_____

_____

_____

_____

Puzzle 3-26

AP BQXHGHTX HT A QMFTBP VOB TXAFXT A
PMV UHMX BP XOAPYTLHWHPL UAK.

—HFW YEQJHPMX

_____

_____

_____

_____

answers on page 253

Puzzle 3-27

XUNF XB'HB HBNTTD FNTVEPA NCYQF ER N
XYPLBHSQT LND RBF NRELB YP FUB SYQHFU
FUQHRLND YS PYWBICBH XUBP PY YPB
LEBFR. E IBNP, XUD BTRB XYQTL FUBD ZNTT
EF FUNPVRAEWEPA?

—BHIN CYICBZV

_____

_____

_____

_____

_____

_____

_____

_____

_____

_____

_____

answer on page 253

Puzzle 3-28

JGKGKWGJ FOQ'M WOLZPI TZ PYG IGHJ. MPJTZF PYG EGHJUM OD YTM DHCOJ. YTQG PYG QHJX EHJPM, GANGEP MO DHJ HM PYGI HJG WJGHXTZF OLP TZ UTFYP! FTCG PYTM OZG QHI PO PYHZXM, PO SOI, PO FJHPTPLQG!

—YGZJI RHJQ WGGNYGJ

_____

_____

_____

_____

_____

_____

_____

_____

_____

_____

answer on page 253

HINTS

Puzzle 3-1: The word "journey" is found in this puzzle.

Puzzle 3-2: The word "born" is found in this puzzle.

Puzzle 3-3: The word "cake" is found in this puzzle.

Puzzle 3-4: The word "begin" is found in this puzzle.

Puzzle 3-5: The word "presents" is found in this puzzle.

Puzzle 3-6: The word "white" is found in this puzzle.

Puzzle 3-7: The word "softer" is found in this puzzle.

Puzzle 3-8: The word "date" is found in this puzzle.

Puzzle 3-9: The word "brings" is found in this puzzle.

Puzzle 3-10: The word "pages" is found in this puzzle.

Puzzle 3-11: The word "know" is found in this puzzle.

Puzzle 3-12: The word "holly" is found in this puzzle.

Puzzle 3-13: The word "happy" is found in this puzzle.

Puzzle 3-14: The word "come" is found in this puzzle.

Puzzle 3-15: The word "child" is found in this puzzle.

Puzzle 3-16: The word "sight" is found in this puzzle.

Puzzle 3-17: The word "who" is found in this puzzle.

Puzzle 3-18: The word "graves" is found in this puzzle.

Puzzle 3-19: The word "rather" is found in this puzzle.

Puzzle 3-20: The word "souls" is found in this puzzle.

Puzzle 3-21: The word "goes" is found in this puzzle.

Puzzle 3-22: The word "year" is found in this puzzle.

Puzzle 3-23: The word "until" is found in this puzzle.

Puzzle 3-24: The word "which" is found in this puzzle.

Puzzle 3-25: The word "love" is found in this puzzle.

Puzzle 3-26: The word "starts" is found in this puzzle.

Puzzle 3-27: The word "diets" is found in this puzzle.

Puzzle 3-28: The word "bounty" is found in this puzzle.

CHAPTER 4

Laughing Out Loud

A good dose of humor is a great way to break up your day. And who better to deliver those punch lines but Woody Allen, Steve Martin, Lucille Ball, Bill Cosby, and George Burns? You'll find some great one-liner quotations from their routines and television shows, or witty sayings they delivered in conversations with others.

WOODY ALLEN

Puzzle 4-1

W SIC'D MQCD DI QXAWOBO WTTIHDQNWDR
DAHIVKA TR MIHZ . . . W MQCD DI QXAWOBO
WD DAHIVKA CID SRWCK.

_____

_____

_____

Puzzle 4-2

V UWWK F JCQQM-HQFMVTD ZWAHJQ FTM
HQFM NFH FTM CQFZQ VT UNQTUX YVTAUQJ.
VU VTSWPSQJ HAJJVF.

_____

_____

_____

answers on page 253

Puzzle 4-3

PWNKA JH GKLLKR LTUN FWVKRLA, JZ WNXA
ZWR ZJNUNOJUX RKUHWNH.

_____

_____

_____

_____

Puzzle 4-4

G'O UFQK LQBCP BV OK EBRP LBTDFX SJXTY.
OK EQJIPVJXYFQ, BI YGN PFJXYAFP, NBRP OF
XYGN SJXTY.

_____

_____

_____

_____

answers on page 253

VZDSGSADVZHXW, YLLFGCVZH DF KFCSGZ
YADGFZFKSGA, ATYLS VA MVZVDS. DQVA
VA Y OSGW LFKMFGDVZH DQFRHQD —
TYGDVLRXYGXW MFG TSFTXS EQF LYZ
ZSOSG GSKSKJSG EQSGS DQSW QYOS XSMD
DQVZHA.

_____

_____

_____

_____

_____

_____

_____

_____

_____

_____

_____

answer on page 254

Puzzle 4-6

AZDK WP QOKZWQC GNWJKJ DQU AG'LG DVV
WQ JOBGHOUT'J ULGDB? OL AZDK'J AOLJG,
AZDK WP OQVT KZDK PDK CRT WQ KZG KZWLU
LOA GNWJKJ?

_____

_____

_____

_____

_____

_____

_____

_____

_____

_____

answer on page 254

LUCILLE BALL

Puzzle 4-7

MLV IVRXVM GJ IMUPZET PGNET ZI MG FZYV
LGEVIMFP, VUM IFGDFP, UEH FZV UKGNM PGNX
UTV.

_____

_____

_____

_____

Puzzle 4-8

IKMA ZK LZQ XZUA, AFANB DEK ZQ AKSZSXAP
SI UEXX DEPXB ZK XIFA YZSL E TINTAIVQ
NAPLAEP.

_____

_____

_____

_____

answers on page 254

Puzzle 4-9

SVX UWW JXCB JVRW VL SVXR CBHENRWK
VKCW ZBWS EWFAW BVJW.

_____

_____

_____

_____

Puzzle 4-10

BGYE'J H NHLUZED, HLC ATJD FTTM JZXQEMJ
HME JDHMRGLS DT CEHDO!

_____

_____

_____

_____

answer on page 254

Puzzle 4-11

IMWCMT, TQ. B ZWL LIX UQY LMCMYWS XMWYL
BT GX MWYSX OWXL BT IQSSXZQQO ATEBS B
UBHAYMO QAE EIWE TQ QTM YMWSSX HWCM
W OWGT BU B ZWL LIX QY TQE, WTO B HQE
QCMY GX LIXTMLL.

_____

_____

_____

_____

_____

_____

_____

_____

_____

_____

answer on page 254

Puzzle 4-12

D BSJP SL PJPORISR OPUDGDHL EBSE FHOVM CHO NP. UHJP RHXOMPUC CDOME, SLI PJPOREBDLG PUMP CSUUM DLEH UDLP.

_____

_____

_____

_____

_____

_____

_____

_____

_____

_____

_____

answer on page 254

GEORGE BURNS

Puzzle 4-13

X'E UBDONU HN B WBXPFUN BD TSGNDOXLQ X PSRN DOBL B TFAANTT BD TSGNDOXLQ X OBDN.

_____

_____

_____

_____

Puzzle 4-14

QFBYQFWFZB HB JYNBI-AYUF YJ QYMYVXTRXJ. CSFZ Y CHJ JYNBI-AYUF Y JBYTT SHM GYWGTFJ.

_____

_____

_____

_____

answers on page 254

Puzzle 4-15

JLUUARPGG AG JLWARI L OLEIP, OFWARI, MLEARI, MOFGP-TRAC SLYAOV AR LRFCJPE MACV.

_____

_____

_____

_____

Puzzle 4-16

VIA'W HWBP QA GKV, LATKHH PIL CBA OBRK OIAKP QA GKV.

_____

_____

_____

_____

answers on page 254

Puzzle 4-17

CLOWF TYG CYOZHF REPHW, FSHR TYG CYOZHF
CEBHW. RHJF TYG CYOZHF FY UGVV TYGO
NLUUHO GU ERQ, CLREVVT, TYG CYOZHF FY
UGVV LF QYXR.

_____

_____

_____

_____

_____

_____

_____

_____

_____

_____

_____

answer on page 255

Puzzle 4-18

VIG UJIQ VIG'BT RTKKAJR IFX QSTJ VIG YKIIL KI
KAT VIGB YSITFMETY MJX QIJXTB QSMK TFYT
VIG EIGFX XI QSAFT VIG'BT XIQJ KSTBT.

_____

_____

_____

_____

_____

_____

_____

_____

_____

answer on page 255

BILL COSBY

Puzzle 4-19

OTXZUJZAAC LV QJUXUDCLDY XZU QJUVUDX
RAF EABU IAVX LV VATQ-AD-T-JAQU.

_____

_____

_____

_____

Puzzle 4-20

PCFCZCMHUCJI NHR UJJ THIG VLZSQ OJV TS,
QJ C RCR TG YSQU UJ VSDVCUS UNST.

_____

_____

_____

_____

answers on page 255

Puzzle 4-21

F AC NWRKAFUYP UDK AU ALKBDRFKP DU YDHW
OWNALVW KBWRW ARW UD ALKBDRFKFWV DU
YDHW, JLVK KBDVW QBD'HW BAS YLNI QFKB
FK AUS KBDVW QBD BAHWU'K.

_____

_____

_____

_____

_____

_____

_____

_____

_____

_____

_____

answer on page 255

Puzzle 4-22

WSD GDZ UBWSD TSXBDO VB ZNHHSQSDV
RYSJNSR GDZ JBWWMDNJGVNBD TSVUSSD
VCSW NR RVNXX ND NVR NDHGDJP.

_____

_____

_____

_____

_____

_____

_____

_____

_____

_____

_____

_____

answer on page 255

Puzzle 4-23

CD BOHHZQ SDP ROFBFM MDJ HQM HD QZYZQZZ, AOQZCHKCT PKFF ZWZCHJOFFM AQDXJRZ LKNOQQZ LZSOWKDQ, OCX K'B CDH HOFVKCT OLDJH HSZ VKXI. HSZKQ LZSOWKDQ KI OFPOMI CDQBOF.

_____

_____

_____

_____

_____

_____

_____

_____

_____

_____

_____

answer on page 255

STEVE MARTIN

Puzzle 4-24

TGE NG WJCH J WLIILGF VGIIJQA: OLQAN, RHN
J WLIILGF VGIIJQA.

_____

_____

_____

_____

Puzzle 4-25

KZO LXZS QETQ NZZL SZWBX DBQ SEBX QEBK
STXQ ABI? WB XBVQEBU.

_____

_____

_____

_____

answers on page 255

Puzzle 4-26

AFLM DQ L ZUXDT QMLN? L ZUXDT QMLN DQ ZLVY MFDVPQ. MFTY RLV WT MLBB, QFUNM, MFDV, UN QEDVVY. MFTY RLV WT GTZURNLMQ . . . UN QEDVVY.

_____

_____

_____

_____

_____

_____

_____

_____

_____

_____

_____

answer on page 255

Puzzle 4-27

VGHQH XD OWH VGXWB X MOCRJ AQHIE CP OYHQ IWJ VGIV XD XZ DGH FICBGV SH MXVG IWOVGHQ MOSIW. X MOCRJW'V DVIWJ ZOQ VGIV.

_____

_____

_____

_____

_____

_____

_____

_____

_____

_____

_____

answer on page 255

Puzzle 4-28

RQD SHQV VZNL RQDG IGQCOTK JY, JL'Y LZNL RQD ZNFTH'L YTTH THQDBZ KQFJTY — NOO QM OJMT'Y GJAAOTY NGT NHYVTGTA JH LZT KQFJTY.

_____

_____

_____

_____

_____

_____

_____

_____

_____

_____

_____

_____

answer on page 255

HINTS

Puzzle 4-1: The word "through" is found in this puzzle.

Puzzle 4-2: The word "twenty" is found in this puzzle.

Puzzle 4-3: The word "poverty" is found in this puzzle.

Puzzle 4-4: The word "proud" is found in this puzzle.

Puzzle 4-5: The word "finite" is found in this puzzle.

Puzzle 4-6: The word "dream" is found in this puzzle.

Puzzle 4-7: The word "about" is found in this puzzle.

Puzzle 4-8: The word "life" is found in this puzzle.

Puzzle 4-9: The word "once" is found in this puzzle.

Puzzle 4-10: The word "banquet" is found in this puzzle.

Puzzle 4-11: The word "several" is found in this puzzle.

Puzzle 4-12: The word "everyday" is found in this puzzle.

Puzzle 4-13: The word "love" is found in this puzzle.

Puzzle 4-14: The word "five" is found in this puzzle.

Puzzle 4-15: The word "family" is found in this puzzle.

Puzzle 4-16: The word "make" is found in this puzzle.

Puzzle 4-17: The word "first" is found in this puzzle.

Puzzle 4-18: The word "while" is found in this puzzle.

Puzzle 4-19: The word "most" is found in this puzzle.

Puzzle 4-20: The word "them" is found in this puzzle.

Puzzle 4-21: The word "just" is found in this puzzle.

Puzzle 4-22: The word "species" is found in this puzzle.

Puzzle 4-23: The word "always" is found in this puzzle.

Puzzle 4-24: The word "million" is found in this puzzle.

Puzzle 4-25: The word "when" is found in this puzzle.

Puzzle 4-26: The word "star" is found in this puzzle.

Puzzle 4-27: The word "break" is found in this puzzle.

Puzzle 4-28: The word "enough" is found in this puzzle.

CHAPTER 5

Get Inspired

Motivational quotations are a thought-provoking way to get fired up about your life and make some needed changes. They also work to promote positive thinking and help you achieve success in the workplace, your relationships, and your personal life. By stimulating your brain to solve these puzzles, you'll enrich your life with quotations from such inspirational people as Winston Churchill, Martin Luther King, Jr., Ralph Waldo Emerson, Mahatma Gandhi, and more.

WINSTON CHURCHILL

Puzzle 5-1

GKZNXAUTTO D'R UTPUON ZKUMO YX TKUZA, UTYJXBSJ D MX AXY UTPUON TDCK WKDAS YUBSJY.

_____

_____

_____

_____

Puzzle 5-2

YMUUKYY PY ALK OBPWPAS AI QI VJIZ ICK VOPWMJK AI OCIALKJ HPAL CI WIYY IV KCALMYPOYZ.

_____

_____

_____

_____

answers on page 256

Puzzle 5-3

O DEWWNZNWM WEEW MHE SNLLNJIPMB NU EXEGB FDDFGMIUNMB; OU FDMNZNWM WEEW MHE FDDFGMIUNMB NU EXEGB SNLLNJIPMB.

_____

_____

_____

_____

_____

_____

_____

_____

_____

_____

answer on page 256

Puzzle 5-4

NQV JAAWLFJVWUUK LHMNSUQ JGQE HOQ
HEMHO, SMH NJLH JZ HOQN TFAR HOQNLQUGQL
MT WVX OMEEK JZZ WL FZ VJHOFVI QGQE
OWTTQVQX.

_____

_____

_____

_____

_____

_____

_____

_____

_____

_____

_____

answer on page 256

RALPH WALDO EMERSON

Puzzle 5-5

JK FKC EK XRBZB CRB LTCR DTW ABTJ, EK SFHCBTJ XRBZB CRBZB SH FK LTCR TFJ ABTVB T CZTSA.

_____

_____

_____

_____

Puzzle 5-6

ISR XZ RQSBR VSA BAH KNVSA KSII; RQSBR RPSV BZ EJ RPSY KSQS QSBI. DSQPBDZ RPSY BQS.

_____

_____

_____

_____

answers on page 256

Puzzle 5-7

P NOACS CGCJM LS EASC AT MOC YPI AJ
ROANO RC OPGC CJNLVJMCZCY P DAJY MOPM
TMPZMECY VT.

_____

_____

_____

_____

Puzzle 5-8

WDP RPGFRY CO F WDVIM GPXX YCIP, VN WC
DFBP YCIP VW.

_____

_____

_____

_____

answers on page 256

Puzzle 5-9

UKCU DKFEK DL PLYGFGU FQ ZSFQW TLESRLG
LCGFLY OSY BG US ZS; QSU UKCU UKL QCUBYL
SO UKL UKFQW FUGLAO FG EKCQWLZ, TBU
UKCU SBY PSDLY US ZS FG FQEYLCGLZ.

_____

_____

_____

_____

_____

_____

_____

_____

_____

_____

answer on page 256

MAHATMA GANDHI

Puzzle 5-10

QMRX TU MA FWG KXBX HW DMX HWPWBBWK.
QXTBC TU MA FWG KXBX HW QMRX
AWBXRXB.

_____

_____

_____

_____

Puzzle 5-11

IZF GFKI HVU IR DMCE URLJKFWD MK IR WRKF
URLJKFWD MC IZF KFJTMAF RD RIZFJK.

_____

_____

_____

_____

answers on page 256

Puzzle 5-12

LXBBAUD CZ TUQ KUXQW WGJCTI CL CQ
AUBZ TUQ CTMRPAB QWB LXBBAUD QU DGNB
DCZQGNBZ.

_____

_____

_____

_____

Puzzle 5-13

AEQZQWQU BJV SUQ MJZRUJZLQO AKLE SZ
JDDJZQZL, MJZYVQU EKG AKLE FJWQ.

_____

_____

_____

_____

answers on pages 256–257

Puzzle 5-14

KG KM HDMJ HVCSTI GC EH QWKHVURJ GC
CVH'M QWKHVUM. ESG GC EHQWKHVU GIH CVH
PIC WHTDWUM IKOMHRQ DM JCSW HVHOJ KM
GIH FSKVGHMMHVXH CQ GWSH WHRKTKCV.
GIH CGIHW KM OHWH ESMKVHMM.

_____

_____

_____

_____

_____

_____

_____

_____

_____

_____

answer on page 257

MARTIN LUTHER KING, JR.

Puzzle 5-15

LZH ATXQU KQWTS JL QSI JMQ IGV RQ KQELNQ
UTAQSJ GKLZJ JMTSWU JMGJ NGJJQH.

_____

_____

_____

_____

Puzzle 5-16

RP OXCJ BPGNL JV BMHP JVAPJTPN GC
UNVJTPNC VN YPNMCT JVAPJTPN GC SVVBC.

_____

_____

_____

_____

answers on page 257

Puzzle 5-17

FI LPM MIK, UM UFVV DMJMJTMD IEL LPM
UEDKQ ER EAD MIMJFMQ, TAL LPM QFVMISM
ER EAD RDFMIKQ.

_____

_____

_____

_____

Puzzle 5-18

K DQFAKC CM JMQ CBEC KY E AEG BEDG'C
OKDUMNVIVO DMAVCBKGP BV TKLL OKV YMI,
BV KDG'C YKC CM LKNV.

_____

_____

_____

_____

answers on page 257

Puzzle 5-19

JHJDWONFW CLK OJ EDJLU . . . OJCLQTJ LKWONFW CLK TJDHJ. WNQ FNK'U MLHJ UN MLHJ L CNXXJEJ FJEDJJ UN TJDHJ. WNQ FNK'U MLHJ UN ZLAJ WNQD TQOIJCU LKF HJDO LEDJJ UN TJDHJ. WNQ NKXW KJJF L MJLDU PQXX NP EDLCJ. L TNQX EJKJDLUJF OW XNHJ.

---

answer on page 257

MOTHER TERESA

Puzzle 5-20

K QYND HFSLP EQD MYAYPFX EQYE KH K RFND
SLEKR KE QSAEW, EQDL EQDAD KW LF QSAE,
OSE FLRB TFAD RFND.

_____

_____

_____

_____

Puzzle 5-21

SAH DY YDA AIAT QYKA HY MYP CFHZYPH
SAXIFDG EAHHAT XDL ZXUUFAT.

_____

_____

_____

answers on page 257

Puzzle 5-22

S FPKR AKE RSNN PKU ASXJ DJ MPIUYSPA S
ZMP'U YMPENJ. S TQHU RSHY UYMU YJ ESEP'U
UGQHU DJ HK DQZY.

_____

_____

_____

_____

Puzzle 5-23

BZ KL EJCL WX OLJDL, BP BU FLDJYUL KL
EJCL ZXVMXPPLW PEJP KL FLQXWM PX LJDE
XPELV.

_____

_____

_____

_____

answers on page 257

Puzzle 5-24

XFY KT VMUF BRF SBDRY, YQMY WF VFFY FMZQ
BYQFI WDYQ M TVDXF, WQFR DY DT GDJJDZKXY
YB TVDXF. TVDXF MY FMZQ BYQFI, VMUF YDVF
JBI FMZQ BYQFI DR ABKI JMVDXA.

_____

_____

_____

_____

_____

_____

_____

_____

_____

_____

_____

answer on page 257

OTHER MOTIVATIONAL QUOTATIONS

Puzzle 5-25

GVHE KXGTA SXG SBHH MBTY PGBVP KGG ODM

UDV QGTTBJHE OBVI GFK XGS ODM GVA UDV PG.

—K. T. AHBGK

_____

_____

_____

_____

Puzzle 5-26

BQI VRTEGIM RZ W BQRTXWGS UALIX UTXB

KIOAG PABQ W XAGOLI XBIY.

—LWR BJT

_____

_____

_____

_____

answers on page 258

Puzzle 5-27

KS KYQHXBR US B OXN, UW XPXY B SFUZXW, ZX
QAUIFR VBQH HAX OKSH US B FUPKYO HAUIOAH
KYHU HAX AXBWH US B SWKXYR, HABH ZUIFR
GX OKPKYO BQ HAX BYOXFQ OKPX.

—OXUWOX NBVRUYBFR

_____

_____

_____

_____

_____

_____

_____

_____

_____

_____

answer on page 258

Puzzle 5-28

SNNH MGMW RBXT HNXHKN GDX CBW CX JNKYCCKN WXPB MTJYCYXZO. OTMKK HNXHKN MKGMWO FX CDMC, JPC CDN BNMKKW EBNMC TMSN WXP RNNK CDMC WXP, CXX, VMZ JNVXTN EBNMC.

—TMBS CGMYZ

_____

_____

_____

_____

_____

_____

_____

_____

_____

answer on page 258

HINTS

Puzzle 5-1: The word "learn" is found in this puzzle.

Puzzle 5-2: The word "failure" is found in this puzzle.

Puzzle 5-3: The word "pessimist" is found in this puzzle.

Puzzle 5-4: The word "pick" is found in this puzzle.

Puzzle 5-5: The word "path" is found in this puzzle.

Puzzle 5-6: The word "real" is found in this puzzle.

Puzzle 5-7: The word "chief" is found in this puzzle.

Puzzle 5-8: The word "have" is found in this puzzle.

Puzzle 5-9: The word "persist" is found in this puzzle.

Puzzle 5-10: The word "live" is found in this puzzle.

Puzzle 5-11: The word "find" is found in this puzzle.

Puzzle 5-12: The word "does" is found in this puzzle.

Puzzle 5-13: The word "love" is found in this puzzle.

Puzzle 5-14: The word "regards" is found in this puzzle.

Puzzle 5-15: The word "begin" is found in this puzzle.

Puzzle 5-16: The word "brothers" is found in this puzzle.

Puzzle 5-17: The word "silence" is found in this puzzle.

Puzzle 5-18: The word "live" is found in this puzzle.

Puzzle 5-19: The word "serve" is found in this puzzle.

Puzzle 5-20: The word "hurts" is found in this puzzle.

Puzzle 5-21: The word "leaving" is found in this puzzle.

Puzzle 5-22: The word "much" is found in this puzzle.

Puzzle 5-23: The word "peace" is found in this puzzle.

Puzzle 5-24: The word "smile" is found in this puzzle.

Puzzle 5-25: The word "those" is found in this puzzle.

Puzzle 5-26: The word "miles" is found in this puzzle.

Puzzle 5-27: The word "flower" is found in this puzzle.

Puzzle 5-28: The word "people" is found in this puzzle.

CHAPTER 6

Going to the Movies

Everyone loves a good movie and a good movie quotation. In this chapter, you'll probably see some of your favorite expressions and learn some new ones. You might even find yourself saying them to your coworkers and friends! Enjoy solving these puzzles with lines from action and adventure movies, comedies, musicals, dramatic and romantic movies, classic movies, and some personal quotations from actors and directors about being in the business.

PERSONAL QUOTATIONS

Puzzle 6-1

U CDKXXULER NUW UKXQWO ONE WUXE
CREEMQX UW U BQPEKDWO NUW GNEB NE
VJYW NDXWEKC WQXE ZUZER.

—WOUBKEY LJVRDAL

_____

_____

_____

_____

Puzzle 6-2

W'R OUP C JFCN RUKWF YPCJ. W'KF YPWNN
ZUP PAF YCRF GWBF W YPCJPFQ UEP GWPA
PGFOPM-FWZAP MFCJY CZU.

—GWNN JUZFJY

_____

_____

_____

_____

answers on page 258

Puzzle 6-3

HIEBVK RQV R FRD. RUDBVLAVK QVRWWG JRLX
XI KVV WBEV RAXIQK IL R KXRCV.

—AORQWBV AORZWBL

_____

_____

_____

_____

Puzzle 6-4

YI   WB   IYCW   WESTF   ZJT   WZXT   UTXFZJ
WYFTXEKCT, Y'QT LZJT WB AZK.

—GZZLB ECCTJ

_____

_____

_____

_____

answers on page 258

Puzzle 6-5

CHMZ VE WUQVZ, CHMZ VE ZYEHD. KP VUX
AVEEQE PYU DPKEDHQKDQ HK XLQ RVS
CHMZ WPQE, VKW GPQE WHUQDXMS XP PYU
CQQMHKGE, WQQA WPRK HKXP XLQ WVUN
UPPZE PC PYU EPYME.

—HKGZVU TQUGZVK

_____

_____

_____

_____

_____

_____

_____

_____

_____

_____

answer on page 258

ACTION/ADVENTURE MOVIES

Puzzle 6-6: *Pulp Fiction*

JG QP WAKNFVK GVJYRHFA PLX HRFA PLX
KRLXUE SFWKF WKBJAY KSWVP OXFKHJLAK.

— KWQXFU U. IWSBKLA

_____

_____

_____

_____

Puzzle 6-7: *Armageddon*

TVL QRFTLJ WTHTLW YSZLURXLRT BQWT
HWALJ QW TS WHZL TVL ISUDJ. HRKSRL IHRRH
WHK RS?

— GUQML IFDDFW

_____

_____

_____

_____

answers on page 259

Puzzle 6-8: *Star Wars*

PST WBLMT RJ OSHP ERVTJ H FTAR SRJ
DBOTL. RP'J HX TXTLEU WRTKA MLTHPTA
NU HKK KRVRXE PSRXEJ. RP JQLLBQXAJ QJ
HXA DTXTPLHPTJ QJ. RP NRXAJ PST EHKHYU
PBETPSTL.

—HKTM EQRXXTJJ

_____

_____

_____

_____

_____

_____

_____

_____

_____

_____

answer on page 259

Puzzle 6-9: *Crouching Tiger Hidden Dragon*

FGL FGHPCE YL FRODG GIWL PR SLKQIPLPDL.
QX QIEFLK YROUA EIX: FGLKL HE PRFGHPC
YL DIP GRUA RPFR HP FGHE YRKUA. RPUX BX
ULFFHPC CR DIP YL FKOUX SREELEE YGIF HE
KLIU.

—DGRY XOP JIF

_____

_____

_____

_____

_____

_____

_____

_____

_____

_____

_____

answer on page 259

ANIMATED MOVIES

Puzzle 6-10: *Pocahontas*

VUX WPNHG WPZ UHLV IZUILZ TPU OSZ IZUILZ,
OSZ WPZ IZUILZ TPU LUUG OHY WPNHG LNGZ
VUX.

—DXYV GXPH

_____

_____

_____

_____

Puzzle 6-11: *Tarzan*

Y OFI PJJ RTJGJ'P PX VHOT RX WJFGI, YR'P
FWW PX OWXPJ FIU CJR PX MFG.

—RXIC SXWULCI

_____

_____

_____

_____

answers on page 259

Puzzle 6-12: *The Little Mermaid*

CAAGEIAKD! CBAS CBFGU CBAS UGPJ AOAKSCBFGI. SPR IFOA CBAN EG FGHB, CBAS DJFN ELL POAK SPR.

—DENRAL A. JKFIBC

_____

_____

_____

_____

Puzzle 6-13: *Finding Nemo*

CAQ TCAYA, MY. KYIMUQ KPLLE. DCAZ LPFA KATE QRI ORDZ OR QRI DXZZX HZRD DCXT QRI'VA KRTTX OR?

—ALLAZ OAKAZAYAE

_____

_____

_____

_____

answers on page 259

Puzzle 6-14: *Winnie the Pooh*

ZATKTWTK EATM JF, NCR ZANETWTK ANHHTCD
EF EATI NVFCJ EAT ZNM, UC EATUK TCPANCETR
HVNPT FC EFH FQ EAT QFKTDE, N VUEEVT
XTNK ZUVV NVZNMD XT ZNUEUCJ.

— DTXNDEUNC PNXFE

_____

_____

_____

_____

_____

_____

_____

_____

_____

_____

answer on page 259

CLASSIC MOVIES

Puzzle 6-15: *Casablanca*

NMGRO AZI FZV AZIV BZFFYY, SYUXRZV.
U SMGQQ DUSS NMGN KMYR KY QYGEY
BGSGPQGRBG.

        —URXVUJ PYVXDGR

_____

_____

_____

_____

Puzzle 6-16: *Some Like It Hot*

RN'S NVP SNKBG KU QG TRUP. R JTDJGS CPN
NVP UHEEG PXL KU NVP TKTTRAKA.

        —QJBRTGX QKXBKP

_____

_____

_____

_____

answers on pages 259–260

Puzzle 6-17: *The Big Sleep*

VFQHE DTE FDTHF BQTRH VQ VFTQB DV D CDM,
EHYEXWDAAS BFEM FE'H BDAKWMZ QPV QO
SQPT UERTQQC.

—FPCYFTES UQZDTV

_____

_____

_____

_____

Puzzle 6-18: *The Quiet Man*

XUSKS'JJ MS IF JFATN FK MFJXN MSXZSSI ON,
RVKQ TVXS . . . SYASHX XUFNS LI QFOK FZI
RSKASIVKQ JLXXJS USVKX!

—DFUI ZVQIS

_____

_____

_____

_____

answers on page 260

COMEDIES

Puzzle 6-19: *Ferris Bueller's Day Off*

AIMR UEXRQ PDRJJW MBQJ, IM WEZ HEN'J
QJEP BNH AEET BDEZNH ENLR IN B OGIAR WEZ
LEZAH UIQQ IJ.

—UBJJGRO YDEHRDILT

_____
_____
_____
_____

Puzzle 6-20: *Men in Black*

MBU PSBD YGE QWRREOESKE IEYDEES MBU
NSQ TE? W TNPE YGWV LBBP XBBQ!

—DWLL VTWYG

_____
_____
_____
_____

answers on page 260

Puzzle 6-21: *Caddyshack*

U'Q ZPXXT ZUIC KPB T RUEERC TOIUGC. EWCYC'M T FPYGC UX EWC BXUICYMC EWTE QTSCM EWUXZM WTHHCX, TXO TRR KPB WTIC EP OP UM ZCE UX EPBGW JUEW UE. MEPH EWUXSUXZ, RCE EWUXZM WTHHCX, TXO NC EWC NTRR.

—GWCIK GWTMC

_____

_____

_____

_____

_____

_____

_____

_____

_____

_____

answer on page 260

Puzzle 6-22: *My Big Fat Greek Wedding*

QCR HRU HEV GR QCR CREF PI QCR CPMTR
GMQ QCR OPHRU EKR QCR URWJ EUF QCRV
WEU QMKU QCR CREF EUV OEV QCRV OEUQ.

—DENUNR JELEU

_____

_____

_____

_____

_____

_____

_____

_____

_____

_____

_____

_____

answer on page 260

DRAMATIC/ROMANTIC MOVIES

Puzzle 6-23: *The Princess Bride*

ZCIF CW VSCN, HCMHNFWW. SNLYNF JHY WSLW
DCIIFBFNKZL CW WFZZCNM WYEFKHCNM.

—USBL FZJFW

_____

_____

_____

_____

Puzzle 6-24: *Good Will Hunting*

UFCM MHKK EK HAMW VHKKENMF ITFA WHY
MHPF KHLFXTEAB LHUF XTCA WHY MHPF
WHYUKFMZ.

—UHNEA IEMMECLK

_____

_____

_____

_____

answers on page 260

Puzzle 6-25: *Cast Away*

QY HROY GNE QY ERY CX ZRFY. GNE QY FWIZ
NVZ BVFFRZ ZLY IRN VD HVIRNU VWA ZAGBK
VN ZRFY.

—ZVF LGNKI

_____

_____

_____

_____

Puzzle 6-26: *The English Patient*

BTBDJ XKEWC K ZIC YIC LJ WBNDC. HIC KX
CWB LYDXKXE KC SNP MIVV NENKX.

—DNVRW MKBXXBP

_____

_____

_____

_____

answers on page 260

MUSICALS

Puzzle 6-27: *Moulin Rouge*

XITU? YQITU YXX SZJDGW J QUXJUTU JD
XITU. XITU JW XJVU ICPGUD. XITU JW Y LYDP-
WRXUDAIEUA SZJDG, XITU XJOSW HW HR
BZUEU BU QUXIDG, YXX PIH DUUA JW XITU.
                                    —UBYD LMGEUGIE

_____
_____
_____
_____
_____
_____
_____
_____
_____
_____
_____

answer on page 261

Puzzle 6-28: *The Wizard of Oz*

CQ C AOAJ HP GPPNCFH QPJ YB XAZJW'R
IARCJA ZHZCF, C SPF'W GPPN ZFB QVJWXAJ
WXZF YB PSF MZTN BZJI. MATZVRA CQ CW
CRF'W WXAJA, C FAOAJ JAZGGB GPRW CW WP
MAHCF SCWX! CR WXZW JCHXW?

—DVIB HZJGZFI

_____

_____

_____

_____

_____

_____

_____

_____

_____

_____

_____

answer on page 261

HINTS

Puzzle 6-1: The word "same" is found in this puzzle.

Puzzle 6-2: The word "years" is found in this puzzle.

Puzzle 6-3: The word "movies" is found in this puzzle.

Puzzle 6-4: The word "done" is found in this puzzle.

Puzzle 6-5: The word "dream" is found in this puzzle.

Puzzle 6-6: The word "scary" is found in this puzzle.

Puzzle 6-7: The word "asked" is found in this puzzle.

Puzzle 6-8: The word "field" is found in this puzzle.

Puzzle 6-9: The word "touch" is found in this puzzle.

Puzzle 6-10: The word "like" is found in this puzzle.

Puzzle 6-11: The word "close" is found in this puzzle.

Puzzle 6-12: The word "swim" is found in this puzzle.

Puzzle 6-13: The word "life" is found in this puzzle.

Puzzle 6-14: The word "along" is found in this puzzle.

Puzzle 6-15: The word "your" is found in this puzzle.

Puzzle 6-16: The word "end" is found in this puzzle.

Puzzle 6-17: The word "throw" is found in this puzzle.

Puzzle 6-18: The word "bolts" is found in this puzzle.

Puzzle 6-19: The word "moves" is found in this puzzle.

Puzzle 6-20: The word "good" is found in this puzzle.

Puzzle 6-21: The word "force" is found in this puzzle.

Puzzle 6-22: The word "neck" is found in this puzzle.

Puzzle 6-23: The word "pain" is found in this puzzle.

Puzzle 6-24: The word "more" is found in this puzzle.

Puzzle 6-25: The word "time" is found in this puzzle.

Puzzle 6-26: The word "night" is found in this puzzle.

Puzzle 6-27: The word "lifts" is found in this puzzle.

Puzzle 6-28: The word "begin" is found in this puzzle.

CHAPTER 7

It's All Politics

Politics run back through the ages and can even be seen in the form of dominance hierarchies or pecking orders in various animal species. The puzzles you'll be solving in this chapter are related to politics and are quotations from famous kings and queens, prime ministers, U.S. presidents and vice presidents, and world leaders. Some of the quotations are political in nature, offer advice on ruling and leadership, or are just humorous and silly.

KINGS AND QUEENS

Puzzle 7-1

E APSZ E FVUH CFH XSBR SQ V ZHVA VPB
QHHXOH ZSIVP, XTC E FVUH CFH FHVWC VPB
DCSIVMF SQ V AEPJ.

—GTHHP HOEYVXHCF E

_____

_____

_____

_____

Puzzle 7-2

DA BKA RIY PRYAKALYAV PR YMA
GILLPNPOPYPAL IF VAFABY; YMAW VI RIY AXPLY.

—HJAAR TPZYIKPB

_____

_____

_____

answers on page 261

Puzzle 7-3

C UDI D QTMMO, DOF SLT VLLG DUDS JS KBLUO;
D UCWM, DOF SLT GCPPMF JS HTIRDOF;
D JLVHMB, DOF SLT FMABCNMF JM LW JS
KHCPFBMO. JS RPLLF DPLOM BMJDCOI: VDGM
CV, RTV FL OLV JDGM JM ITWWMB PLOX.

—JDBCM DOVLCOMVVM

_____

_____

_____

_____

_____

_____

_____

_____

_____

_____

_____

answer on page 261

Puzzle 7-4

MABEJNS FJJIF LD HJ FD IQVU LUJ FLNGMGAC
RJBLQNJ DR GLF [BIJNGVB'F] GAUBHGLBALF
LUBL GL IBS ADL GA LUJ JAT HJ BA JEGW LUBL
LUJS KGWW HJVDIJ BWGJAF LD LUJ MGACTDI.
—MGAC CJDNCJ GGG

_____

_____

_____

_____

_____

_____

_____

_____

_____

_____

_____

answer on page 261

PRIME MINISTERS

Puzzle 7-5

FSD ERU'A GUTKDVUEV VDLSBV'O TDADLV
TLSX AHV AVLLREVO. FSD HRIV AS CV SU AHV
BGAEH RUQ BKRFGUJ HRLQ.

—NSHU XRNSL

_____

_____

_____

_____

Puzzle 7-6

XPY WBCO YAAYOXCBRA KU B AGSSYAAUGR
MHCWY WCOCAXYH [BHY] ARYYM BOI B AYOAY
KU PCAXKHN.

—PBHKRI DCRAKO

_____

_____

_____

_____

answers on page 261

Puzzle 7-7

R IHRVHG SWMX BRFH XBH JPWGRKH XP RJX
RKRUZMX RZ HQYHGX'M RVFUJH.

—ARSHM JRIIRKBRZ

_____

_____

_____

Puzzle 7-8

X LXEE KQZ AEE CB QRUZMSRO RV IUXMS
AIVKR A JKQR QVFXZRB RV A MARXVM EXHXMS
XM A RVKSO LVUET.

—WXZUUZ ZEEXVRR RUKTZAK

_____

_____

_____

answers on page 262

Puzzle 7-9

OX HLFPAC HXXW GS KAA NXKDH VD FPZ BFOXZ TF KIFVC OKZ, GS KDKASHVDY BFHHVGAX JKPHXH, GS TZSVDY TF ZXNFIX TLXN, GS CVHJPHHVFD VD K HBVZVT FM JFAAKGFZKTVFD KDC YFFC OVAA.

—DXIVAAX JLKNGXZAKVD

_____

_____

_____

_____

_____

_____

_____

_____

_____

_____

answer on page 262

U.S. PRESIDENTS

Puzzle 7-10

GYHALJG LO XKT GXNTZLXP LI LT JKXOLOTO
KI HGJZ KI BO. LT LO OKYHTZLXP KXDN LI LT
JKXOLOTO KI GDD KI BO.

—UKKVAKU ULDOKX

_____

_____

_____

_____

Puzzle 7-11

IWDS, CBSDS XDS KEIBVJSIC NSJ EJ TVYXT
LVHSDJNSJC. PWC CBSDS XDS KEIBVJSIC NSJ
EJ JXCEVJXT LVHSDJNSJC, CVV.

—DEYBXDK JERVJ

_____

_____

_____

_____

answers on page 262

Puzzle 7-12

OGOSM QFT WRIW BY JIEO, OGOSM KISYRBD
UIFTAROE, OGOSM SZANOWLBSOE, YBQTBLBOY
BT I LBTIU YOTYO I WROLW LSZJ WRZYO KRZ
RFTQOS ITE ISO TZW LOE, WRZYO KRZ ISO
AZUE ITE ISO TZW AUZWROE.

—EKBQRW E. OBYOTRZKOS

_____

_____

_____

_____

_____

_____

_____

_____

_____

_____

_____

answer on page 262

Puzzle 7-13

W RYKI NBIVVIE MOB OVMZ BRWN VXYBFMCH
BRYB W HYP NII PMO YZE BRYB PMO HYP NII
HI, YZE WZ BRI YCCYZJIHIZB W RYKI BRI SINB
MF BRI SYCJYWZ.

— YSCYRYH XWZLMXZ

_____

_____

_____

_____

_____

_____

_____

_____

_____

_____

_____

_____

answer on page 262

PRESIDENTIAL JOKES

Puzzle 7-14

R YFIL R'Q DMNNRFD HMNNMU XN DICB
HMPXOSM R'Q TRNNRFD BMLMU SJMPNXNIUS.

—DMUXCG BIUG

_____

_____

_____

_____

Puzzle 7-15

K MDXP UAZPV SDVZPY ZU YCUSV EG
ZCUBWJPF, WBZ K IDV'Z RPZ EG SKAP ZU RU
FSKEEKVR.

—TKEEG IDCZPC

_____

_____

_____

_____

answers on page 262

Puzzle 7-16

V FLMLH IHVFY DBTTLL JG WSFDO. V TVFI VG
YLLZC UL JRJYL TBH GOL JTGLHFBBF.

—HBFJWI HLJXJF

_____

_____

_____

_____

Puzzle 7-17

MSNKJA RWT CFWT XNVT MSTL RWT KFH MSRK
MSTL TITW HTWT QTEFWT.

—OHNJSM O. TNATKSFHTW

_____

_____

_____

_____

answers on pages 262–263

Puzzle 7-18

GYND GN QHS IDSH HFFIPN, SYN SYIDQ SYWS UEAMAIUNZ CN SYN CHUS GWU SYWS SYIDQU GNAN WU VWZ WU GN'Z VNND UWRIDQ SYNR GNAN.

—KHYD F. ONDDNZR

_____

_____

_____

_____

_____

_____

_____

_____

_____

_____

answer on page 263

U.S. VICE PRESIDENTS

Puzzle 7-19

OQ OV BAVC QG QAJB IOWBEQC XGE TEAFQBY,
SZBF CGD ZAPB FBPBE ZAY OQ QAJBF XEGK
CGD.

—YOHJ HZBFBC

_____

_____

_____

_____

Puzzle 7-20

BXTI TAU GQCVRUXMC TQC TFFXFRUCI FO
BC ZCGF XA LTAU, AOF TFFXFRUCI FO BC
TJOXUCU.

—MLTQWCI MRQFXI

_____

_____

_____

_____

answers on page 263

Puzzle 7-21

GBLREJGV ZECAUBGJN ES LGSN UV WTL
ORGEV OKW TLAA UV WTL QLLW.

—JTGRALS D. ZGXLS

_____

_____

_____

_____

Puzzle 7-22

RHS Q KHPVN SOXJUS MU O WUSGOBX QB XJU
JHPWU HR XJU VHSN XJOB XH WQX QB XJU
WUOXW HR XJU CQAJXY.

—OVMUB K. MOSTVUY

_____

_____

_____

_____

answers on page 263

Puzzle 7-23

THZXVN JHWIAICS AHZQG VXKUIVXS Q TQSAXVG HF AXWXDISIHN. I'DX NXDX V VXQWWG PQVTXZ UJ AH AXWXDISIHN QNZ, IN FQIVNXSS AH AXWXDISIHN, IA'S NXDXV PQVTXZ UJ AH TX.

—PQWAXV F. THNZQWX

answer on page 263

WORLD LEADERS

Puzzle 7-24

XMS QSCU JMU NORLU UMM MNUZJ AOUL MJZ
ZJZQX, MY XMS AOGG UZPBL LOQ PGG XMSY
PYU MN APY.

—JPFMGZMJ IMJPFPYUZ

_____

_____

_____

_____

Puzzle 7-25

BTYHJHFA HA WLP WHJUTIJ NYTTVAUXV,
WUHYX WLP HA BTYHJHFA WHJU NYTTVAUXV.
—KLT JAX-JIZS

_____

_____

_____

_____

answers on page 263

Puzzle 7-26

P JUI RXCNJF WI VYUIF UZ P GJPBI DXIYI UV
DUJJ PVVYPBV VXI PVVIZVUCZ CT VXI DCYJF.

—PYUIJ RXPYCZ

_____

_____

_____

_____

Puzzle 7-27

XIV AXVQ IXL QVYY LFV VNOLF HDXI GFWRF
LFV DVXDYV GNYP.

—RONMT FXOQV

_____

_____

_____

_____

answers on pages 263–264

Puzzle 7-28

PB SMGPEPYX PE PX BHYHXXWJI HPEQHJ EM
CHEJWI MBH'X YMABEJI MJ EQH HGHYEMJWEH.
P SJHLHJ EM CHEJWI EQH HGHYEMJWEH.

—YQWJGHX VH NWAGGH

_____

_____

_____

_____

_____

_____

_____

_____

_____

_____

_____

_____

answer on page 264

HINTS

Puzzle 7-1: The word "woman" is found in this puzzle.

Puzzle 7-2: The word "not" is found in this puzzle.

Puzzle 7-3: The word "suffer" is found in this puzzle.

Puzzle 7-4: The word "kingdom" is found in this puzzle.

Puzzle 7-5: The word "hard" is found in this puzzle.

Puzzle 7-6: The word "prime" is found in this puzzle.

Puzzle 7-7: The word "courage" is found in this puzzle.

Puzzle 7-8: The word "tough" is found in this puzzle.

Puzzle 7-9: The word "should" is found in this puzzle.

Puzzle 7-10: The word "consists" is found in this puzzle.

Puzzle 7-11: The word "local" is found in this puzzle.

Puzzle 7-12: The word "hunger" is found in this puzzle.

Puzzle 7-13: The word "best" is found in this puzzle.

Puzzle 7-14: The word "getting" is found in this puzzle.

Puzzle 7-15: The word "drown" is found in this puzzle.

Puzzle 7-16: The word "lunch" is found in this puzzle.

Puzzle 7-17: The word "like" is found in this puzzle.

Puzzle 7-18: The word "saying" is found in this puzzle.

Puzzle 7-19: The word "liberty" is found in this puzzle.

Puzzle 7-20: The word "kept" is found in this puzzle.

Puzzle 7-21: The word "easy" is found in this puzzle.

Puzzle 7-22: The word "seats" is found in this puzzle.

Puzzle 7-23: The word "warmed" is found in this puzzle.

Puzzle 7-24: The word "teach" is found in this puzzle.

Puzzle 7-25: The word "politics" is found in this puzzle.

Puzzle 7-26: The word "world" is found in this puzzle.

Puzzle 7-27: The word "earth" is found in this puzzle.

Puzzle 7-28: The word "either" is found in this puzzle.

CHAPTER 8

Religion and Spirituality

Religion may be shared by a large community or may be very personal. There are many interpretations of what religion is, but it typically includes an object of devotion and a method of proper behavior in regard to how you live your life and relate to the world around you. The cryptograms you'll be solving in this chapter include quotations related to Christianity, Judaism, Buddhism, Confucianism, and Native American spirituality; there are also general quotations about religion and God.

ABOUT RELIGIOUS BELIEF

Puzzle 8-1

PZ GHJ NEDUVDJ RW PY KPW HMY PLUGD, MD
KUFD LHED VKUY EDNPBEHNUVDJ.

—FHIVUPED

_____

_____

_____

_____

Puzzle 8-2

T NKBTKEK TX WUJ BTIK T NKBTKEK TX SQK
FHXRTFK. XUS NKPLHFK T PLX FKK TS, NHS
NKPLHFK T PLX FKK LBB SQLS TS SUHPQKF.

—P. F. BKZTF

_____

_____

_____

_____

answers on page 264

Puzzle 8-3

D KOFFZR KZFKGDSG ZRJGVEDHG RJOF RJOR JG, RJG DFLDFDRG LORJGV, GUMGKRH ZV VGXPDVGH FZ EZVHJDM ZV MVODHG LVZW PH, NPR RJOR JG DH GSGF DFLDFDRGQY ONZSG DR.

—NGFCOWDF LVOFAQDF

_____
_____
_____
_____
_____
_____
_____
_____
_____
_____
_____

answer on page 264

TEACHINGS OF BUDDHA

Puzzle 8-4

BMDVUMZ KDZM BEZ WDBY, JDZVU BEZ YMOVU
XOB MZOPM ELZ FEEY YMMYP.

_____

_____

_____

_____

Puzzle 8-5

MVLJ QVUM CR DJAOCVLR. CZ CR VLJ YATCONA
EVJ GIGXAFCFK. ZJAGZ CZ ICZT OGJA.

_____

_____

_____

_____

answers on page 264

Puzzle 8-6

AN INSINCERE AND EVIL FRIEND IS MORE

AL OLFOLRSYS ALG SHOV EYOSLG OF BQYS

TO BE FEARED THAN A WILD BEAST A WILD

KQ DS ESAYSG KUAL A COVG DSAFK; A COVG

BEAST MAY WOUND YOUR BODY BUT AN EVIL

DSAFK BAI CQNLG IQNY DQGI, DNK AL SHOV

FRIEND WILL WOUND YOUR MIND

EYOSLG COVV CQNLG IQNY BOLG.

_____

_____

_____

_____

_____

_____

_____

_____

_____

_____

answer on page 264

CONFUCIAN THOUGHT

Puzzle 8-7

U DABP BQT U CKPEAS. U LAA BQT U PAWAWYAP.
U TK BQT U VQTAPLSBQT.

_____

_____

_____

_____

Puzzle 8-8

FXS'G SMAUVXG MVX MNIBX, IA IG APXIV
PMRIAG APMA YMVVJ APXF QMV MLMVA.

_____

_____

_____

_____

answers on page 264

Puzzle 8-9

FG JBB CISF HJ OHNIF, SWD WGF FG DG HF, HJ CSWF GQ MGEOSNB GO GQ UOHWMHUTB.

_____

_____

_____

_____

Puzzle 8-10

EN CEG WXNPQW CMZEGJZ SGYNWZF CMLL BMAY MZ YMBBMVJLZ ZG SPQN EMW CGUYW DGGY.

_____

_____

_____

_____

answers on pages 264–265

Puzzle 8-11

QGXO WDF MODQ K NGIOC, ND GDVA NGKN
WDF MODQ IN; KOA QGXO WDF AD ODN MODQ
K NGIOC, ND KVVDQ NGKN WDF AD ODN MODQ
IN — NGIY IY MODQVXACX.

_____

_____

_____

_____

_____

_____

_____

_____

_____

_____

answer on page 265

NATIVE AMERICAN SPIRITUALITY

Puzzle 8-12

GIY ANXKMO XM UIBSI UY ZGVMO BZ
ZVSNYO ANXKMO. BG BZ GIY FCXXO XT XKN
VMSYZGXNZ.

—SIBYT WCYMGR SXKWZ

_____

_____

_____

_____

Puzzle 8-13

THE
SGI LWDI XWO NVWT, SGI LWDI XWO TBMM
T   T   THE
SDORS YVH SGI MIRR XWO TBMM CIYD.

—WUBPTYX

_____

_____

_____

_____

answers on page 265

Puzzle 8-14

FHDWD ERBW QDMQXD WDDG GVMUXDEKD,
VMF UIWEMO. GVMUXDEKD IW ML FHD QRWF,
UIWEMO IW ML FHD LCFCND.

—XCOSDD

_____

_____

_____

_____

Puzzle 8-15

IZL FUX DZAI DTQNK HY UXZPXQ JOHD KHYFOL
SBHQ FUTK UHIX ZQN FUX MAXZF KBTATF
JOXKK ZOO DUH XQFXA.

—RUXAHWXX JOXKKTQM

_____

_____

_____

answers on page 265

Puzzle 8-16

OZWD GRB OWNW FRND, GRB MNUWP HDP
SZW ORNEP NWJRUMWP. EUAW GRBN EULW
TR SZHS OZWD GRB PUW, SZW ORNEP MNUWT
HDP GRB NWJRUMW.

—OZUSW WEC

_____

_____

_____

_____

_____

_____

_____

_____

_____

_____

_____

answer on page 265

THE BIBLE

Puzzle 8-17

IE TUBLQ, TUA QEZ AO UOZ NCU; AO UOZ DEZ
ZSE NYU BO AOFU OU QOYL TUBEL.

_____

_____

_____

_____

Puzzle 8-18

PG MIUG GUEDYO TO ZGM NGMVP ETRD
GUEDYO PG MIUG ZGM.

_____

_____

_____

_____

answers on page 265

Puzzle 8-19

HKQ ADR LSMM WKDL XTB XERXT, HKQ XTB XERXT LSMM JHWB ADR UEBB.

_____

_____

_____

_____

Puzzle 8-20

GHCS ML VUPMSQP UQX OMQX; GHCS ML QHP DSUGHFL HK THULPJFG; MP ML QHP UKKHZUQP HK KFXS.

_____

_____

_____

_____

answers on page 265

THE KORAN

Puzzle 8-21

PJ SQJVIJH XVY. PJ KYGP IAJ DQGXDIMYZB GW
AMB BGFN, VYH VQJ SNGBJQ IG AMX IAVY IAJ
EJMY GW AMB YJSK.

_____

_____

_____

_____

Puzzle 8-22

EZ UDO HCK GTJKAWKSKOZ, HCKWO VDOBZ
EOK AWBK E RWOEIK WT E XKZKOH.

_____

_____

_____

_____

answers on pages 265–266

Puzzle 8-23

RW IRCI FRQQHWH C LWSZPZQT QYWL ZHSCA,
ZI EZSS TQI GW CFFWUIWO JLQA RZA CTO ZT
IRW EQLSO IQ FQAW RW EZSS GW QTW QJ IRW
SQHI.

_____

_____

_____

_____

_____

_____

_____

_____

_____

_____

_____

answer on page 266

Puzzle 8-24

WQAWRVF, LMCV SMQ AK FRV EKYVOJVUVQN
MKX FRV RDWAZQJFVN MKX XVMO
QJBAQAENOD SJFR FRVL. RVOO NRMOO YV
FRVJQ RALV: MK VUJO IMFV.

_____

_____

_____

_____

_____

_____

_____

_____

_____

_____

answer on page 266

THE TALMUD

Puzzle 8-25

KQCGEQ DL JDD ZFRB XGFOBJQE, LDE
PJ SQGSQTV JBQ ZPTS GTS HEDSFRQV
DKXPUPDT.

_____

_____

_____

_____

Puzzle 8-26

JKE LRW GAEIMNI RWQ QEMN WEI, TN RW
RLLEYGUTLM TW IKM RLI.

_____

_____

_____

_____

answers on page 266

Puzzle 8-27

C WTYZUB AGJJ MT ICJJTS NU CIIUHBN UB
RHSEDTBN SCQ PUY TFTYQ WTYDGZZGMJT
NKGBE KT DGEKN KCFT TBRUQTS MHN SGS
BUN.

_____

_____

_____

_____

_____

_____

_____

_____

_____

_____

_____

_____

answer on page 266

Puzzle 8-28

DCVQ WV QGZ VACT YKTTV QGZ LAIU, VA RAI YKTTV QGZ NAFTI. DCVQ WV QGZ VACT LZWFV QGZ LAIU, VA RAI ZMICFZV QGZ NAFTI. DCVQ WV QGZ VACT VZZV LCQ KV MAQ VZZM, VA RAI VZZV LCQ KV MAQ VZZM.

_____

_____

_____

_____

_____

_____

_____

_____

_____

_____

_____

answer on page 266

HINTS

Puzzle 8-1: The word "than" is found in this puzzle.

Puzzle 8-2: The word "touches" is found in this puzzle.

Puzzle 8-3: The word "expects" is found in this puzzle.

Puzzle 8-4: The word "birth" is found in this puzzle.

Puzzle 8-5: The word "body" is found in this puzzle.

Puzzle 8-6: The word "feared" is found in this puzzle.

Puzzle 8-7: The word "and" is found in this puzzle.

Puzzle 8-8: The word "alike" is found in this puzzle.

Puzzle 8-9: The word "want" is found in this puzzle.

Puzzle 8-10: The word "modesty" is found in this puzzle.

Puzzle 8-11: The word "when" is found in this puzzle.

Puzzle 8-12: The word "ground" is found in this puzzle.

Puzzle 8-13: The word "more" is found in this puzzle.

Puzzle 8-14: The word "people" is found in this puzzle.

Puzzle 8-15: The word "winds" is found in this puzzle.

Puzzle 8-16: The word "live" is found in this puzzle.

Puzzle 8-17: The word "angry" is found in this puzzle.

Puzzle 8-18: The word "unto" is found in this puzzle.

Puzzle 8-19: The word "make" is found in this puzzle.

Puzzle 8-20: The word "jealous" is found in this puzzle.

Puzzle 8-21: The word "created" is found in this puzzle.

Puzzle 8-22: The word "mirage" is found in this puzzle.

Puzzle 8-23: The word "world" is found in this puzzle.

Puzzle 8-24: The word "fate" is found in this puzzle.

Puzzle 8-25: The word "laughter" is found in this puzzle.

Puzzle 8-26: The word "act" is found in this puzzle.

Puzzle 8-27: The word "might" is found in this puzzle.

Puzzle 8-28: The word "sees" is found in this puzzle.

CHAPTER 9

Scientific Discoveries

Where in the world would we be without science? An interesting thought to ponder. Science is made up of many fields of study, including biology, chemistry, physics, and mathematics. Within these fields you'll find scientists who are performing research to further explore and explain their area of expertise. And, of course, out of this research new discoveries and inventions often arise! In this chapter you'll find quotations about the various areas of scientific study and statements from famous scientists about their work and views.

THE STUDY OF LIFE

Puzzle 9-1

F LDGYRDA FANOLH RM HQO HQORGB RM
OCRZDHYRJ YA HQFH OCOGBERUB HQYJPA QO
DJUOGAHFJUA YH.

—KFLTDOA IRJRU

_____

_____

_____

_____

Puzzle 9-2

CAHVTVU EXLI HXIW BCVUV EXI JV AQ JVMLN
XPMTV, MB MW FVUBXML BCXB BCVUV XUV
TXWBPI EAUV HXIW AQ JVMLN SVXS.

—UMFCXUS SXHYMLW

_____

_____

_____

_____

answers on page 266

Puzzle 9-3

JXOFOYB XA RLM AEXMTEM OI FXIM XT DFF
XRA QDTXIMARDRXOTA DTW XA RLM UMB RO
DFF OGN IGRGNMA.

—WDSXW JMFFDQB

_____

_____

_____

_____

Puzzle 9-4

ADABC   FBAZJ   ZXDZHVA   UH   HZJYBZM
PHRKMAXFA GZW UHDRMDAX JGA ZSWRMYJA
BANAVJURH RT ZYJGRBUJC.

—JGROZW GAHBC GYQMAC

_____

_____

_____

_____

answers on page 266

Puzzle 9-5

QPSMZRBST, KR MQKVR BT RGQ VQTVQ RGKR
HKCLBT VIQKDV SJ BR, XKTTSR FQ HQRQXRQH
LBRGBT RGQ MBJQRBOQ SJ K VBTYMQ
SFVQCPQC.

—HKPBH F. DBRRV

_____

_____

_____

_____

_____

_____

_____

_____

_____

_____

answer on page 267

CHEMICAL PROPERTIES

Puzzle 9-6

RKUSEHNMV EH B NMBQU DCM ZUCZLU IENKCPN UXCPOK ESBOEXBNECX NC TU ZKVHEREHNH.

—BMNKPM R. RLBMYU

_____

_____

_____

_____

Puzzle 9-7

YAW AWSWE AYBNZWT UCHB CHT GWWA IYAW; YAW ZHA YAPL TWW UCHB EWDHNAT BY GW IYAW.

—DHENW ZFENW

_____

_____

_____

_____

answers on page 267

Puzzle 9-8

SZ S LOPH O JLFIEOVK SKHOE OVK FVAT FVH
JIXVE FIJ JF MH DFFK, S OB EOJSEZSHK.

                        —OAZXHK MHXVLOXK

_____

_____

_____

_____

Puzzle 9-9

UF EAZ YSJJVZ RVZFSF TUZDUZQIV, Q JZSFJ
KACF TAZV JLUI KLVTQFJF.

                         —WAUI DSFFAC

_____

_____

_____

_____

answers on page 267

Puzzle 9-10

VB, DZYF DGYTR SBV'D SBGR . . . ZBS BV ELGDZ
LGE QBK EOEG PBYVP DB EANMLYV YV DEGCF
BW TZECYFDGQ LVI NZQFYTF FB YCNBGDLVD L
UYBMBPYTLM NZEVBCEVBV LF WYGFD MBOE?
—LMUEGD EYVFDEYV

_____

_____

_____

_____

_____

_____

_____

_____

_____

_____

answer on page 267

INVENTIONS AND INVENTORS

Puzzle 9-11

EPF JOLOEBR GFDTRAEOTY OK MBG NTGF
KOLYOMOZBYE EPBY EPF OYDFYEOTY TM
SGOEOYL TG FDFY TM XGOYEOYL.

—JTALRBK FYLFRHBGE

_____

_____

_____

_____

Puzzle 9-12

N ARCWJEE SVXS N EXNU SR HK OIRSVJI
RIZNMMJ SVXS HXC LRPMU CRS WMK WRI
WNWSK KJXIE.

—LNMOPI LINQVS

_____

_____

_____

_____

answers on page 267

Puzzle 9-13

EALQ WQL UWWT BMWHLH SQWYALT UWWT
WZLQH; PKY EL HW WNYLQ MWWO HW MWQR
SQU HW TLRTLYNKMMX KZWQ YAL BMWHLU
UWWT, YASY EL UW QWY HLL YAL WQLH EAVBA
WZLQ NWT KH.

—SMLFSQULT RTSASC PLMM

_____

_____

_____

_____

_____

_____

_____

_____

_____

_____

_____

answer on page 267

Puzzle 9-14

JQLWY XMZVE PWBYBLFMPWS. VXNFMDV
JQLWY. MTXQFV QY. JBKV QY. NAY MNBKV
MJJ, ZCBO JQLWY. ZCBO QY HBF MJJ SBA MFV
OBFYW, MCT SBA OQJJ ZCBO YWV ZVS YB
PWBYBLFMPWS.

—LVBFLV VMEYXMC

_____

_____

_____

_____

_____

_____

_____

_____

_____

_____

answer on page 267

PLAYING WITH NUMBERS

Puzzle 9-15

R ORQTKORQHZHRM HJ R PAHMN ORM HM
R NRVU VCCO ACCUHMD ECV R PARZU ZRQ
GTHZT HJM'Q QTKVK.

—ZTRVAKJ NRVGHM

_____

_____

_____

_____

Puzzle 9-16

FBNBMS AFBHY HUS, NPE EUJ BFKS EUJBXZJY
HUZWU HBXA RXJ EUJ QREUJQREZWRK BFJY.

—QZWURJK UBKE

_____

_____

_____

_____

answers on page 268

Puzzle 9-17

PXC RQPXCRQPMUQB NUMCDUCN
KQTPMUHBQTBI CEXMWMP VTJCT, NIRRCPTI,
QDJBMRMPQPMVD; QDJ PXCNC QTC PXC
YTCQPCNP LVTRN VL PXC WCQHPMLHB.

       —QTMNPVPBC

_____

_____

_____

_____

_____

_____

_____

_____

_____

_____

answer on page 268

Puzzle 9-18

MN SMU MN LCA QMBN WS FMLCAFMLRDN UASAU LW UAMQRLX, LCAX MUA VWL DAULMRV; MVG MN SMU MN LCAX MUA DAULMRV, LCAX GW VWL UASAU LW UAMQRLX.

—MQJAUL ARVNLARV

_____

_____

_____

_____

_____

_____

_____

_____

_____

_____

_____

answer on page 268

PHYSICS AND THE UNIVERSE

Puzzle 9-19

WNZM FL EFOS? OD EZMMPA.
WNZM FL EZMMPA? OPUPA EFOS.
          —MNDEZL NPWFMM XPR

_____

_____

_____

_____

Puzzle 9-20

BR XPT YBZG WP SOFC ON OHHDC HBC WLTDX
RLPS ZJLOWJG, XPT STZW RBLZW BNUCNW
WGC TNBUCLZC.
          —JOLD ZOION

_____

_____

_____

_____

answers on page 268

Puzzle 9-21

IYXVX DVX CONK IGC IVLNK EOREOEIX IYEOPS,
IYX LOEMXVSX DOU SILJEUEIK. DOU E DF
LOSLVX DHCLI IYX LOEMXVSX.

—DNHXVI XEOSIXEO

_____

_____

_____

_____

Puzzle 9-22

VS MTGUVYU, GIP WIS'D TNLH DI ZI NFIPSW
JNEVSZ DFIPAQH RIF GIPFUHQR — SNDPFH
WIHU VD RIF GIP.

—RFNSE BVQYCHE

_____

_____

_____

_____

answers on page 268

BUT EBTI UBC, QX SUBKWUA HDD CVT
ZVXIWMHD DHKI HI KT SUBK CVTF CBEHX,
WFFTEWHCTDX BQCHWU HU RUETNIC
HUEWUA BJ HUXCVWUA FRMV.

—NWMVHNE Z. JTXUFHU

_____

_____

_____

_____

_____

_____

_____

_____

_____

_____

_____

answer on page 268

DOING RESEARCH

Puzzle 9-24

HNCH'B HNY ECHPXY OM XYBYCXRN — JOP
IOE'H LEOQ QNCH WE NYSS JOP'XY IOWEU.
—NCXOSI "IOR" YIUYXHOE

_____

_____

_____

_____

Puzzle 9-25

YMQMJYSI RQ AIM JSA FV KFRCK GD JPPMNQ
AF QMM RV AIMN JYM OPRCB.
—DPGAJYSI

_____

_____

_____

_____

answers on pages 268–269

Puzzle 9-26

FU MLZ WNDXS UKLT LAD XZNVLK, FN'W
GSXBFXKFWT; FU MLZ WNDXS UKLT TXAM,
FN'W KDWDXKOV.

—PFSWLA TFRADK

_____

_____

_____

_____

Puzzle 9-27

SOVYW GBVBOGWZ YV XZOP Y'C RFYMT XZBM
Y RFM'P JMFX XZOP Y'C RFYMT.

—XBGMZBG UFM SGOQM

_____

_____

_____

_____

answers on page 269

Puzzle 9-28

XGM CRXUCAM CL HDE NMFZCRN FMNMHFUG UHD CDYE WM XC AHKM XTC VRMNXZCDN JFCT TGMFM CDYE CDM JFMT WMLCFM.

—XGCFNXMZD SMWYMD

_____

_____

_____

_____

_____

_____

_____

_____

_____

answer on page 269

HINTS

Puzzle 9-1: The word "theory" is found in this puzzle.

Puzzle 9-2: The word "alive" is found in this puzzle.

Puzzle 9-3: The word "key" is found in this puzzle.

Puzzle 9-4: The word "involved" is found in this puzzle.

Puzzle 9-5: The word "single" is found in this puzzle.

Puzzle 9-6: The word "enough" is found in this puzzle.

Puzzle 9-7: The word "remains" is found in this puzzle.

Puzzle 9-8: The word "turns" is found in this puzzle.

Puzzle 9-9: The word "cows" is found in this puzzle.

Puzzle 9-10: The word "trick" is found in this puzzle.

Puzzle 9-11: The word "more" is found in this puzzle.

Puzzle 9-12: The word "years" is found in this puzzle.

Puzzle 9-13: The word "closed" is found in this puzzle.

Puzzle 9-14: The word "worth" is found in this puzzle.

Puzzle 9-15: The word "blind" is found in this puzzle.

Puzzle 9-16: The word "only" is found in this puzzle.

Puzzle 9-17: The word "forms" is found in this puzzle.

Puzzle 9-18: The word "reality" is found in this puzzle.

Puzzle 9-19: The word "what" is found in this puzzle.

Puzzle 9-20: The word "wish" is found in this puzzle.

Puzzle 9-21: The word "unsure" is found in this puzzle.

Puzzle 9-22: The word "trouble" is found in this puzzle.

Puzzle 9-23: The word "physical" is found in this puzzle.

Puzzle 9-24: The word "know" is found in this puzzle.

Puzzle 9-25: The word "going" is found in this puzzle.

Puzzle 9-26: The word "many" is found in this puzzle.

Puzzle 9-27: The word "basic" is found in this puzzle.

Puzzle 9-28: The word "outcome" is found in this puzzle.

CHAPTER 10

Playing Sports

Sports are a great way to blow off steam, build your competitive spirit, and work on developing your physical skills. There are many different sports to choose from, and you can take lessons, join a team, play with your children, watch an event on TV, join a crowd at a stadium, or even bet on the outcome! The puzzles you'll be solving in this chapter will give you insight and tips into the worlds of baseball, basketball, football, golf, hockey, and tennis.

BASEBALL

Puzzle 10-1

B NLSU AQHP AQU OYZUIOMBMBAQ. MAYJN
LHH MNU DLOUO GNUQ B NBM L NAEU IYQ.

—DLDU IYMN

_____

_____

_____

_____

Puzzle 10-2

ZGBDNDA ZQVUT UB RVBZ UGD GDQAU QVI
WOVI BF QWDAOEQ GQI MDUUDA CDQAV
MQTDMQCC.

—LQESKDT MQAYKV

_____

_____

_____

_____

answers on page 269

Puzzle 10-3

SVTYSVCC MT UFY EWCO PMYCK EP YWKYVJEA
IFYAY V QVW GVW TBGGYYK UFAYY UMQYT
EBU EP UYW VWK SY GEWTMKYAYK V XEEK
NYAPEAQYA.

—UYK IMCCMVQT

_____
_____
_____
_____
_____
_____
_____
_____
_____
_____

answer on page 269

Puzzle 10-4

REZCREHH XZ GJC VELNKXGC EBCKXIEF ZQNKG RCIEWZC XG'Z ZN ZHNY. EFU XMXNG IEF VNHHNY XG. EFM SWZG ERNWG EFU XMXNG IEF QHEU XG.

—ANKC LXMEH

answer on page 269

BASKETBALL

Puzzle 10-5

VWOFAROFV   D   UTDNFL'V   HLFDAFVA
KMDTTFXHF   RV   KWORXH   AW   HLRUV
SRAM   MRV   WX   AMF   AFDO.

—VKWAARF URUUFX

_____

_____

_____

_____

Puzzle 10-6

CUMQJOCUKK   IM   KIQJ   BAVOVRDUBAN: IZ
NVF   XVT'O   ZVGFM,   UKK   NVF   AUSJ   IM   OAJ
TJRUOISJ.

—XUT ZDIMCN

_____

_____

_____

_____

answers on page 269

Puzzle 10-7

BFL KCF GCF VL C GSIGJCA JFQSLWJLFR BF C
RLCK, VIR BFL KCF GCFFBR KCZL C RLCK.

—ZCSLLK CVWIA-MCVVCS

_____

_____

_____

_____

Puzzle 10-8

ILQF R CNFK, R GNW AHUQWLRFS HF RW. R
IDFW WLQ JDEE WH LRW WLQ TEHHY JQTHYQ
R CH.

—CDYYBE CDIKRFA

_____

_____

_____

_____

answers on page 270

Puzzle 10-9

SYHNEDSYCC MH CMNE VYU MR DXYD
JWWERHMZE VEYKJRH YUE GEZECJKEG
WMUHD, YRG MD YCVYOH DYNEH Y VXMCE
WJU DXE GEWERHE DJ QYDQX BK.

—UEG YBEUSYQX

_____

_____

_____

_____

_____

_____

_____

_____

_____

_____

_____

answer on page 270

FOOTBALL

Puzzle 10-10

ETTYUQPP ECQYVDCO YMT TE YLC MTDOY
QOACZYO TE QFCDNZQG PNEC, JNTPCGZC
QGW ZTFFNYYCC FCCYNGKO.

—KCTDKC MNPP

_____

_____

_____

_____

Puzzle 10-11

IJO UZM MBC XBITQZIO Z WBBIFZAA IOZX TN IB
OATXTHZIO IJO CHXBITQZIOL BHON.

—ABC JBAIY

_____

_____

_____

_____

answers on page 270

Puzzle 10-12

FAH EBCG OA RPBF OEIU NBVG PIXG UAVGKAZF
WHUO EIO FAHS VAOEGS MIOE B OMA-KF-
LAHS.

—ZBT KISZMGPP

_____

_____

_____

_____

Puzzle 10-13

VXXHBQLL GTA'H Q PXHHQPH TIXNH, GH'T Q
PXLLGTGXA TIXNH. SQAPGAZ GT Q PXHHQPH
TIXNH.

—SJVVC SQJZYUNHC

_____

_____

_____

_____

answers on page 270

Puzzle 10-14

MAIL XLAXEL RWYVT HAARPOEE YM O IORRLQ
AH EYHL OVF FLORW. Y FAV'R EYTL RWOR
ORRYRUFL. Y BOV OMMUQL RWLI YR YM IUBW
IAQL MLQYAUM RWOV RWOR.

—PYEE MWOVTEJ

_____

_____

_____

_____

_____

_____

_____

_____

_____

_____

answer on page 270

GOLF

Puzzle 10-15

SGIN LW RAY BGWR NKQ ZGK HJQ AJPY
XLRAGKR RJFLQS ZGKE HIGRAYW GNN.

—HAL HAL EGOELSKYD

_____

_____

_____

_____

Puzzle 10-16

FL OIC ENFGV FE'T NBYA EI KXXE GXD MXIMPX,
EYO MFRVFGH CM ENX DYIGH HIPL JBPP.

—ZBRV PXKKIG

_____

_____

_____

_____

answers on page 270

Puzzle 10-17

RE FWI HYS KWRXK ZW ZMYWD H OLIG, RZ RV
RUJWYZHXZ ZW ZMYWD RZ HMSHA WE FWI,
AWDX ZMS EHRYDHF, VW FWI AWX'Z DHVZS
SXSYKF KWRXK GHON ZW JRON RZ IJ.

—ZWUUF GWLZ

answer on page 270

Puzzle 10-18

WARI OUUNORP FA FKN LVLAF LY XP OYV FKN JKLRV. MXPF KAZ JKLRVRLBN WARI UROQNDP CNJAEN LP UDASNY CQ FKNLD IDNHXNYF LYOCLRLFQ FA JAXYF UOPF ILSN.

—MAKY XUVLBN

_____

_____

_____

_____

_____

_____

_____

_____

_____

_____

_____

answer on page 271

HOCKEY

Puzzle 10-19

GCB XDCEQBE NBQFBCI GS IXB WXGIW VGD
EGC'I ILRB EGC'I AG PC.

—JLVCB AQBIHRV

_____

_____

_____

_____

Puzzle 10-20

BYN IFYSNV BL R CFMQ FC PBLFMPNMHV
YFJPTYW BJ KIBYI WIN LYFMN BL SNGW.

—PFTA HRMLFJ

_____

_____

_____

_____

answers on page 271

Puzzle 10-21

E LFQC CZ O WEIBC CBF ZCBFN QEIBC OQS O
BZAUFP IOVF XNZUF ZTC.

—NZSQFP SOQIFNWEFKS

_____

_____

_____

_____

Puzzle 10-22

OCC DGRQBK JCOKBUS OUB AXCXNFVOC.
WDBK QNGI BNFCXSD ONY JUGMONXWK.

—FGUYXB DGIB

_____

_____

_____

_____

answers on page 271

Puzzle 10-23

NTILVW'C O BFXXW EOKV. WTF NOZV YT RPTZV
WTFPCVJB VZVPW CNHBY, VZVPW EOKV. HY'C
XTY FR YT OXWQTDW VJCV. WTF NOZV YT YOLV
RPHDV HX WTFPCVJB.

—ROFJ ITBBVW

answer on page 271

TENNIS

Puzzle 10-24

LWID REOV RB PBV, RB UOY DOXB O NQFQYP;
REOV RB PQFB, EIRBFBW, DOXBZ O NQLB.

—OWVEGW OZEB

_____

_____

_____

_____

Puzzle 10-25

SURMRYX IUTT GTUZT RZ DRAT LDQJRYX
MTYYRZ SRMN MNT YTM BVSY.

—UVPTUM IUVZM

_____

_____

_____

_____

answers on page 271

Puzzle 10-26

HV MOJTOQT MCKM LTQQHM HM QOL
VTJHQHQT, H MCK MRNTU HL.
　　　　　　　　　　—NOMHT RCMCPM

_____

_____

_____

_____

Puzzle 10-27

IMTTXP XP BT BFFXLIXDT IUBI DTLM XI UBP
INHSJ UDDCMF B GBT EXSS TDI SMI UXG YD.
　　　　　　　　　　—NHPPMSS SJTMP

_____

_____

_____

_____

answers on page 271

Puzzle 10-28

XHQQMC WHOYQAC XY XLH
MQNMVMNIUOMCXMK RUCX — U LHSY,
YS UX BYCX U RUMS YG GSMHQNC YS
OYVHSC, UAUMQCX XLH TYSON.

—DUKZIHC WUSEIQ

_____

_____

_____

_____

_____

_____

_____

_____

_____

_____

_____

answer on page 271

HINTS

Puzzle 10-1: The word "touch" is found in this puzzle.

Puzzle 10-2: The word "heart" is found in this puzzle.

Puzzle 10-3: The word "field" is found in this puzzle.

Puzzle 10-4: The word "about" is found in this puzzle.

Puzzle 10-5: The word "team" is found in this puzzle.

Puzzle 10-6: The word "like" is found in this puzzle.

Puzzle 10-7: The word "make" is found in this puzzle.

Puzzle 10-8: The word "dunk" is found in this puzzle.

Puzzle 10-9: The word "first" is found in this puzzle.

Puzzle 10-10: The word "meetings" is found in this puzzle.

Puzzle 10-11: The word "ones" is found in this puzzle.

Puzzle 10-12: The word "just" is found in this puzzle.

Puzzle 10-13: The word "dancing" is found in this puzzle.

Puzzle 10-14: The word "much" is found in this puzzle.

Puzzle 10-15: The word "clothes" is found in this puzzle.

Puzzle 10-16: The word "wrong" is found in this puzzle.

Puzzle 10-17: The word "club" is found in this puzzle.

Puzzle 10-18: The word "proven" is found in this puzzle.

Puzzle 10-19: The word "hundred" is found in this puzzle.

Puzzle 10-20: The word "score" is found in this puzzle.

Puzzle 10-21: The word "broke" is found in this puzzle.

Puzzle 10-22: The word "English" is found in this puzzle.

Puzzle 10-23: The word "game" is found in this puzzle.

Puzzle 10-24: The word "give" is found in this puzzle.

Puzzle 10-25: The word "down" is found in this puzzle.

Puzzle 10-26: The word "say" is found in this puzzle.

Puzzle 10-27: The word "him" is found in this puzzle.

Puzzle 10-28: The word "belongs" is found in this puzzle.

CHAPTER 11

Cryptogram Jumble

This final chapter is packed with great quotes from an eclectic group. Some of the puzzles you'll be solving are inspirational, some are funny, some are religious, some are bizarre—but all are interesting! You'll gain insight from some of the world's most famous writers, actors, athletes, politicians, musicians, comedians, and more. Get your mind moving while decoding these attention-grabbing puzzles, and enjoy!

Puzzle 11-1

RJIIKRR TR MSY YPK VKRJUY SB RWSMYOMKSJR
ISNLJRYTSM. QSJ NJRY RKY QSJVRKUB SM
BTVK.

—VKHHTK UKOIP

_____

_____

_____

_____

Puzzle 11-2

ZJN TEDBHMDKDE IZUBN GOT ZJMNJH ZJN
TIDNDMJOX IZUBN. UB GOFB VJDQBQ PDTTDXBT
OHQ PDTVJDQBQ PBH.

—PONMDH XJMGBN ADHV, YN.

_____

_____

_____

_____

answers on page 272

Puzzle 11-3

S TSPBHHLQCA QN XWBU MQR PBM, YRU XSEE
TANAVT UQ UWA TABUW MQRL LSZWU UQ PBM
SU.

—CQEUBSLA

_____

_____

_____

_____

Puzzle 11-4

YRWV HUE WOK CM PUJ'M PCXV VU HUE. YRWV
HUE TWZK UX HUEOMKAX CM HUEO PCXV DWIZ
VU PUJ.

—ZKAAH QKBBKMKG

_____

_____

_____

_____

answers on page 272

Puzzle 11-5

XNGWLEN HRFB VS BHL'PN XNNR VR JON
MNNTNEJ PWFFNB GWR BHL NPNC URHZ OHZ
AWDRVSVGNRJ VJ VE JH XN HR JON OVDONEJ
AHLRJWVR.

—CVGOWCM A. RVKHR

_____

_____

_____

_____

_____

_____

_____

_____

_____

_____

_____

answer on page 272

Puzzle 11-6

KAZIAWZADD OZI MJZIZADD OWA ZTK DJLZD TX RAOMZADD OZI IADHOJW, NVK COZJXADKOKJTZD TX DKWAZLKU OZI WADTFVKJTZ.

—MOUFJF LJNWOZ

_____

_____

_____

_____

_____

_____

_____

_____

_____

_____

_____

answer on page 272

Puzzle 11-7

GV'H FSFXGCI VMFV VMA FSJWCV JY CAQH VMFV MFTTACH GC VMA QJPOZ AUAPK ZFK FOQFKH BWHV ADFNVOK YGVH VMA CAQHTFTAP.

—BAPPK HAGCYAOZ

_____

_____

_____

_____

_____

_____

_____

_____

_____

_____

_____

_____

answer on page 272

Puzzle 11-8

AUNXN FXN AMV JFYAEWR TNKBNYAY MN OFW
REHN VBX OUEJGXNW. VWN EY XVVAY. AUN
VAUNX EY MEWRY.

      —UVGGEWR OFXANX, SX.

_____

_____

_____

_____

Puzzle 11-9

CPMXGFL, P IPMO, ZA IGKKIL SPVLY PR KULL,
ERO G'II CPMXGFL KUA XMLEK JGX SPVL PR
ZL.

      —MPJLMK CMPYK

_____

_____

_____

_____

answers on page 272

Puzzle 11-10

R NCD LPE MCWS FPLS YMSKS R RLESLBSB EP
FP, AIE R EMRLH R MCWS SLBSB IU YMSKS R
RLESLBSB EP AS.

—BPIFQCT CBCNT

_____

_____

_____

_____

Puzzle 11-11

PZDOA QDI NJEEONN IZD'L EXQDBO MOZMSO;
LXOA POWOSA QPMSYCA VXQL YN QSWOQIA
LXOWO.

—VYSS NPYLX

_____

_____

_____

_____

answers on page 273

Puzzle 11-12

ZCM'HX UXOXH FG NCCS FG XOXHZCUX VXRRG
ZCM JQXU ZCM JEU, FUS ZCM'HX UXOXH FG
PFS FG VQXZ GFZ JQXU ZCM RCGX.

—RCM QCRVT

_____

_____

_____

_____

_____

_____

_____

_____

_____

_____

_____

answer on page 273

Puzzle 11-13

UVC'M PVSSE OLVQM NAVNRA HMAORJCB EVQS JUAOH. JD EVQS JUAOH OSA OCE BVVU, EVQ'RR TOWA MV SOY MTAY UVPC NAVNRA'H MTSVOMH.

—TVPOSU OJGAC

answer on page 273

Puzzle 11-14

N UPEUQT ZMDY ZB ZJV TFBDZT FURVT SNDTZ,
EJNGJ DVGBDHT FVBFPV'T UGGBIFPNTJIVYZT.
ZJV SDBYZ FURV JUT YBZJNYR LMZ IUY'T
SUNPMDVT.

—GJNVS OMTZNGV VUDP EUDDVY

_____

_____

_____

_____

_____

_____

_____

_____

_____

_____

answer on page 273

Puzzle 11-15

GHVKHTNN BMSBPN JRIVMITN HJNC; PVD
LBR'Z NZTBM NTLVRE WBNT BRE CTTG PVDH
AVVZ VR AJHNZ WBNT.

—AHTETHJLC SJMLVY

_____

_____

_____

_____

Puzzle 11-16

BZFV M'P MVTOMAFN, M DFS FGUMSFN
XFUWYTF M UWV'S BWMS SL TFF BZWS
M'RR ULPF YO BMSZ VFGS.

—NLRRC OWASLV

_____

_____

_____

_____

answers on page 273

Puzzle 11-17

JZQGRBD HF WZHOB KERY IZQ RGD RAGRHW
YZ WZ. YEDGD JRO TD OZ JZQGRBD QOSDFF
IZQ'GD FJRGDW.

—DWWHD GHJNDOTRJEDG

_____

_____

_____

Puzzle 11-18

ZNSPYFY YDMYKKYXMY MGXZAZQZ AX
VPYTRAXU QIY YXYFC'Z PYZAZQTXMY
EAQIGNQ LAUIQAXU.

—ZNX-QJN

_____

_____

_____

answers on page 273

Puzzle 11-19

HSB HKQMUDB GYHS SNAYFV NF QJBF WYFI, QO EQMKRB, YR HSNH JBQJDB GYDD YFRYRH QF EQWYFV NDQFV NFI HKZYFV HQ JMH HSYFVR YF YH.

—HBKKZ JKNHESBHH

_____

_____

_____

_____

_____

_____

_____

_____

_____

_____

_____

answer on page 273

Puzzle 11-20

CTA VYG ZTD KDAF GDC ZDNJ LDN CTA EDHA DL
ZDNJ PRC DGEW LDN VDGAW OF GDC EOJAEW
CD VYJA VDGAW GDN LOGK VRST LRG OG
EOLA.

—STYNEAF FSTZYP

_____

_____

_____

_____

_____

_____

_____

_____

_____

answer on page 273

RUAQIXDNB AJFD TX DJBTDN XU CU J MUX UW
XGTZLB, HIX AUBX UW XGD XGTZLB XGDO AJFD
TX DJBTDN XU CU CUZ'X ZDDC XU HD CUZD.
　　　　　　　　　　　—JZCO NUUZDO

_____

_____

_____

_____

_____

_____

_____

_____

_____

_____

answer on page 274

Puzzle 11-22

RA REJV. ZL SEN'FA DEZKD IE WXPA XK AFFEF,
WXPA X VEEHS, XKV VEK'I RA XLFXZV IE UZI
IUA RXJJ.

—RZJJZA QAXK PZKD

_____

_____

_____

_____

Puzzle 11-23

ATASV JSEFKE HFZK LFK PSMKL FB LFK YNB
KYMG, JBH ZJFBEK LFK YNB BJEMSA FBEY LFK
ZFIEMSAK.

—LABSV NJSH PAAILAS

_____

_____

_____

_____

answers on page 274

HINTS

Puzzle 11-1: The word "fire" is found in this puzzle.

Puzzle 11-2: The word "outrun" is found in this puzzle.

Puzzle 11-3: The word "death" is found in this puzzle.

Puzzle 11-4: The word "make" is found in this puzzle.

Puzzle 11-5: The word "highest" is found in this puzzle.

Puzzle 11-6: The word "kindness" is found in this puzzle.

Puzzle 11-7: The word "news" is found in this puzzle.

Puzzle 11-8: The word "wings" is found in this puzzle.

Puzzle 11-9: The word "great" is found in this puzzle.

Puzzle 11-10: The word "where" is found in this puzzle.

Puzzle 11-11: The word "people" is found in this puzzle.

Puzzle 11-12: The word "lose" is found in this puzzle.

Puzzle 11-13: The word "down" is found in this puzzle.

Puzzle 11-14: The word "front" is found in this puzzle.

Puzzle 11-15: The word "keep" is found in this puzzle.

Puzzle 11-16: The word "because" is found in this puzzle.

Puzzle 11-17: The word "courage" is found in this puzzle.

Puzzle 11-18: The word "fighting" is found in this puzzle.

Puzzle 11-19: The word "mind" is found in this puzzle.

Puzzle 11-20: The word "work" is found in this puzzle.

Puzzle 11-21: The word "easier" is found in this puzzle.

Puzzle 11-22: The word "make" is found in this puzzle.

Puzzle 11-23: The word "paints" is found in this puzzle.

Answers

CHAPTER 2: BEAUTY AND FASHION

Puzzle 2-1
A thing of beauty is a joy forever; its loveliness increases; it will never pass into nothingness.

John Keats

Puzzle 2-2
In every man's heart there is a secret nerve that answers to the vibrations of beauty.

Christopher Morley

Puzzle 2-3
Beauty is one of the rare things that do not lead to doubt of God.

Jean Anouilh

Puzzle 2-4
Our hearts are drunk with a beauty our eyes could never see.

George W. Russell

Puzzle 2-5
The beauty that addresses itself to the eyes is only the spell of the moment; the eye of the body is not always that of the soul.

George Sand

Puzzle 2-6
Beauty deprived of its proper foils and adjuncts ceases to be enjoyed as beauty, just as light deprived of all shadows ceases to be enjoyed as light.

John Ruskin

Puzzle 2-7
Remember that always dressing in understated good taste is the same as playing dead.

Susan Catherine

Puzzle 2-8
A woman's dress should be like a barbed-wire fence: serving its purpose without obstructing the view.

Sophia Loren

Puzzle 2-9
Dress simply. If you wear a dinner jacket, don't wear anything else on it . . . like lunch or dinner.

George Burns

Puzzle 2-10
The dress must follow the body of a woman, not the body following the shape of the dress.

Hubert de Givenchy

Puzzle 2-11

Do not trouble yourself much to get new things, whether clothes or friends . . . . Sell your clothes and keep your thoughts.

Henry David Thoreau

Puzzle 2-12

It is new fancy rather than taste which produces so many new fashions.

Voltaire

Puzzle 2-13

Does fashion matter? Always—though not quite as much after death.

Joan Rivers

Puzzle 2-14

I wear my sort of clothes to save me the trouble of deciding which clothes to wear.

Katharine Hepburn

Puzzle 2-15

Fashion is something that goes in one year and out the other.

Denise Klahn

Puzzle 2-16

Fashion is gentility running away from vulgarity, and afraid of being overtaken by it. It is a sign the two things are not far asunder.

William Hazlitt

Puzzle 2-17

My mother insisted that I had to try things on to make sure they were becoming. Becoming what, I always asked.

Edith Konecky

Puzzle 2-18

Ladies of Fashion starve their happiness to feed their vanity, and their love to feed their pride.

Charles Caleb Colton

Puzzle 2-19

Hair style is the final tip-off whether or not a woman really knows herself.

Hubert de Givenchy

Puzzle 2-20

A designer is only as good as the star who wears her clothes.

Edith Head

Puzzle 2-21

I wish I had invented blue jeans. They have expression, modesty, sex appeal, simplicity—all I hope for in my clothes.

Yves Saint Laurent

Puzzle 2-22

Fashion anticipates, and elegance is a state of mind . . . a mirror of the time in which we live, a translation of the future, and should never be static.

Oleg Cassini

Puzzle 2-23

My weakness . . . is architecture. I think of my work as ephemeral architecture, dedicated to the beauty of the female body.

Christian Dior

Puzzle 2-24

Stick to the basics, hold on to your family and friends—they will never go out of fashion.

Niki Taylor

Puzzle 2-25

In the studio, I do try to have a thought in my head, so that it's not like a blank stare.

Cindy Crawford

Puzzle 2-26

In modeling, there is no point in trying to prove you have a brain, so why even bother? I'd sooner save the energy for something more meaningful.

Helena Christensen

Puzzle 2-27

I think most people are curious about what it would be like to be able to meet yourself—it's eerie.

Christy Turlington

Puzzle 2-28

Some people have active imaginations, but they don't know me and they're wrong if they think they do.

Yamila Diaz

CHAPTER 3: HOLIDAY CELEBRATIONS

Puzzle 3-1

A birthday is just the first day of another 365-day journey around the sun. Enjoy the trip!

Author unknown

Puzzle 3-2

You were born an original. Don't die a copy.

John Mason

Puzzle 3-3

You know you are getting old when the candles cost more than the cake.

Bob Hope

Puzzle 3-4

Just remember, once you're over the hill you begin to pick up speed.

Charles Schultz

Puzzle 3-5

There are three hundred and sixty-four days when you might get un-birthday presents . . . and only one for birthday presents, you know.

Lewis Carroll

Puzzle 3-6

My Birthday! what a different sound
That word had in my youthful ears;
And how each time the day comes round,
Less and less white its mark appears.

Thomas Moore

Puzzle 3-7

Christmas waves a magic wand over this world, and behold, everything is softer and more beautiful.

Norman Vincent Peale

Puzzle 3-8

Christmas, children, is not a date. It is a state of mind.

Mary Ellen Chase

Puzzle 3-9

From home to home, and heart to heart, from one place to another. The warmth and joy of Christmas brings us closer to each other.

Emily Matthews

Puzzle 3-10

The rooms were very still while the pages were softly turned and the winter sunshine crept in to touch the bright heads and serious faces with a Christmas greeting.

Louisa May Alcott

Puzzle 3-11

I'm dreaming of a white Christmas,
Just like the ones I used to know.

Puzzle 3-12

Deck the halls with boughs of holly
Fa la la la la la la la la

Puzzle 3-13
We wish you a Merry Christmas,
And a Happy New Year.

Puzzle 3-14
O come, all ye faithful, joyful and triumphant,
Oh come ye, O come ye to Bethlehem.

Puzzle 3-15
Silent night! Holy night!
All is calm, all is bright
Round yon virgin mother and child,
Holy infant so tender and mild,
Sleep in Heavenly peace!

Puzzle 3-16
Have yourself a merry little Christmas.
Let your heart be light,
From now on our troubles
Will be out of sight.

Puzzle 3-17
A grandmother pretends she doesn't know who you are on Halloween.

Erma Bombeck

Puzzle 3-18
At first cock-crow the ghosts must go

Back to their quiet graves below.

Theodosia Garrison

Puzzle 3-19
There is nothing funny about Halloween. This sarcastic festival reflects, rather, an infernal demand for revenge by children on the adult world.

Jean Baudrillard

Puzzle 3-20
Hark! Hark to the wind! 'Tis the night, they say,
When all souls come back from the far away—
The dead, forgotten this many a day!

Virna Sheard

Puzzle 3-21
A New Year's resolution is something that goes in one year and out the other.

Author unknown

Puzzle 3-22
The object of a new year is not that we should have a new year. It is that we should have a new soul.

G. K. Chesterton

Puzzle 3-23

An optimist stays up until midnight to see the new year in. A pessimist stays up to make sure the old year leaves.

Bill Vaughan

Puzzle 3-24

No one ever regarded the First of January with indifference. It is that from which all date their time, and count upon what is left.

Charles Lamb

Puzzle 3-25

This is the finest measure of thanksgiving: a thankfulness that springs from love.

William C. Skeath

Puzzle 3-26

An optimist is a person who starts a new diet on Thanksgiving Day.

Irv Kupcinet

Puzzle 3-27

What we're really talking about is a wonderful day set aside on the fourth Thursday of November when no one diets. I mean, why else would they call it Thanksgiving?

Erma Bombeck

Puzzle 3-28

Remember God's bounty in the year. String the pearls of His favor. Hide the dark parts, except so far as they are breaking out in light! Give this one day to thanks, to joy, to gratitude!

Henry Ward Beecher

CHAPTER 4: LAUGHING OUT LOUD

Puzzle 4-1

I don't want to achieve immortality through my work . . . I want to achieve it through not dying.

Puzzle 4-2

I took a speed-reading course and read War and Peace in twenty minutes. It involves Russia.

Puzzle 4-3

Money is better than poverty, if only for financial reasons.

Puzzle 4-4

I'm very proud of my gold pocket watch. My grandfather, on his deathbed, sold me this watch.

Puzzle 4-5

Interestingly, according to modern astronomers, space is finite. This is a very comforting thought—particularly for people who can never remember where they have left things.

Puzzle 4-6

What if nothing exists and we're all in somebody's dream? Or what's worse, what if only that fat guy in the third row exists?

Puzzle 4-7

The secret of staying young is to live honestly, eat slowly, and lie about your age.

Puzzle 4-8

Once in his life, every man is entitled to fall madly in love with a gorgeous redhead.

Puzzle 4-9

You see much more of your children once they leave home.

Puzzle 4-10

Life's a banquet, and most poor suckers are starving to death!

Puzzle 4-11

Heaven, no. I was shy for several years in my early days in Hollywood until I figured out that no one really gave a damn if I was shy or not, and I got over my shyness.

Puzzle 4-12

I have an everyday religion that works for me. Love yourself first, and everything else falls into line.

Puzzle 4-13

I'd rather be a failure at something I love than a success at something I hate.

Puzzle 4-14

Retirement at sixty-five is ridiculous. When I was sixty-five I still had pimples.

Puzzle 4-15

Happiness is having a large, loving, caring, close-knit family in another city.

Puzzle 4-16

Don't stay in bed, unless you can make money in bed.

Puzzle 4-17
First you forget names, then you forget faces. Next you forget to pull your zipper up and, finally, you forget to pull it down.

Puzzle 4-18
You know you're getting old when you stoop to tie your shoe-laces and wonder what else you could do while you're down there.

Puzzle 4-19
Fatherhood is pretending the present you love most is soap-on-a-rope.

Puzzle 4-20
Civilization had too many rules for me, so I did my best to rewrite them.

Puzzle 4-21
I am certainly not an authority on love because there are no authorities on love, just those who've had luck with it and those who haven't.

Puzzle 4-22
Men and women belong to different species and communication between them is still in its infancy.

Puzzle 4-23
No matter how calmly you try to referee, parenting will eventually produce bizarre behavior, and I'm not talking about the kids. Their behavior is always normal.

Puzzle 4-24
How to make a million dollars: First, get a million dollars.

Puzzle 4-25
You know that look women get when they want sex? Me neither.

Puzzle 4-26
What is a movie star? A movie star is many things. They can be tall, short, thin, or skinny. They can be Democrats . . . or skinny.

Puzzle 4-27
There is one thing I would break up over and that is if she caught me with another woman. I wouldn't stand for that.

Puzzle 4-28
You know what your problem is, it's that you haven't seen enough movies—all of life's riddles are answered in the movies.

CHAPTER 5: GET INSPIRED

Puzzle 5-1
Personally I'm always ready to learn, although I do not always like being taught.

Puzzle 5-2
Success is the ability to go from one failure to another with no loss of enthusiasm.

Puzzle 5-3
A pessimist sees the difficulty in every opportunity; an optimist sees the opportunity in every difficulty.

Puzzle 5-4
Men occasionally stumble over the truth, but most of them pick themselves up and hurry off as if nothing ever happened.

Puzzle 5-5
Do not go where the path may lead, go instead where there is no path and leave a trail.

Puzzle 5-6
Let us treat men and women well; treat them as if they were real. Perhaps they are.

Puzzle 5-7
A chief event of life is the day in which we have encountered a mind that startled us.

Puzzle 5-8
The reward of a thing well done, is to have done it.

Puzzle 5-9
That which we persist in doing becomes easier for us to do; not that the nature of the thing itself is changed, but that our power to do is increased.

Puzzle 5-10
Live as if you were to die tomorrow.

Learn as if you were to live forever.

Puzzle 5-11
The best way to find yourself is to lose yourself in the service of others.

Puzzle 5-12
Freedom is not worth having if it does not include the freedom to make mistakes.

Puzzle 5-13

Whenever you are confronted with an opponent, conquer him with love.

Puzzle 5-14

It is easy enough to be friendly to one's friends. But to befriend the one who regards himself as your enemy is the quintessence of true religion. The other is mere business.

Puzzle 5-15

Our lives begin to end the day we become silent about things that matter.

Puzzle 5-16

We must learn to live together as brothers or perish together as fools.

Puzzle 5-17

In the end, we will remember not the words of our enemies, but the silence of our friends.

Puzzle 5-18

I submit to you that if a man hasn't discovered something he will die for, he isn't fit to live.

Puzzle 5-19

Everybody can be great . . . because anybody can serve. You don't have to have a college degree to serve. You don't have to make your subject and verb agree to serve. You only need a heart full of grace. A soul generated by love.

Puzzle 5-20

I have found the paradox that if I love until it hurts, then there is no hurt, but only more love.

Puzzle 5-21

Let no one ever come to you without leaving better and happier.

Puzzle 5-22

I know God will not give me anything I can't handle. I just wish that He didn't trust me so much.

Puzzle 5-23

If we have no peace, it is because we have forgotten that we belong to each other.

Puzzle 5-24

Let us make one point, that we meet each other with a smile, when it is difficult to smile. Smile at each other, make time for each other in your family.

Puzzle 5-25
Only those who will risk going too far can possibly find out how far one can go.

T. S. Eliot

Puzzle 5-26
The journey of a thousand miles must begin with a single step.

Lao Tzu

Puzzle 5-27
If instead of a gem, or even a flower, we should cast the gift of a loving thought into the heart of a friend, that would be giving as the angels give.

George MacDonald

Puzzle 5-28
Keep away from people who try to belittle your ambitions. Small people always do that, but the really great make you feel that you, too, can become great.

Mark Twain

CHAPTER 6: GOING TO THE MOVIES

Puzzle 6-1
A filmmaker has almost the same freedom as a novelist has when he buys himself some paper.

Stanley Kubrick

Puzzle 6-2
I'm not a real movie star. I've still got the same wife I started out with twenty-eight years ago.

Will Rogers

Puzzle 6-3
Movies are a fad. Audiences really want to see live actors on a stage.

Charlie Chaplin

Puzzle 6-4
If my film makes one more person miserable, I've done my job.

Woody Allen

Puzzle 6-5
Film as dream, film as music. No art passes our conscience in the way film does, and goes directly to our feelings, deep down into the dark rooms of our souls.

Ingmar Bergman

Puzzle 6-6

If my answers frighten you then you should cease asking scary questions.

Samuel L. Jackson

Puzzle 6-7

The United States government just asked us to save the world. Anyone wanna say no?

Bruce Willis

Puzzle 6-8

The Force is what gives a Jedi his power. It's an energy field created by all living things. It surrounds us and penetrates us. It binds the galaxy together.

Alec Guinness

Puzzle 6-9

The things we touch have no permanence. My master would say: there is nothing we can hold onto in this world. Only by letting go can we truly possess what is real.

Chow Yun Fat

Puzzle 6-10

You think the only people who are people, are the people who look and think like you.

Judy Kuhn

Puzzle 6-11

I can see there's so much to learn, it's all so close and yet so far.

Tony Goldwyn

Puzzle 6-12

Teenagers! They think they know everything. You give them an inch, they swim all over you.

Samuel E. Wright

Puzzle 6-13

Hey there, Mr. Grumpy Gills. When life gets you down do you wanna know what you've gotta do?

Ellen DeGeneres

Puzzle 6-14

Wherever they go, and whatever happens to them along the way, in their enchanted place on top of the forest, a little bear will always be waiting.

Sebastian Cabot

Puzzle 6-15

Thank you for your coffee, seignor. I shall miss that when we leave Casablanca.

Ingrid Bergman

Puzzle 6-16

It's the story of my life. I always get the fuzzy end of the lollipop.

Marilyn Monroe

Puzzle 6-17

Those are harsh words to throw at a man, especially when he's walking out of your bedroom.

Humphrey Bogart

Puzzle 6-18

There'll be no locks or bolts between us, Mary Kate . . . except those in your own merce-nary little heart!

John Wayne

Puzzle 6-19

Life moves pretty fast, if you don't stop and look around once in a while you could miss it.

Matthew Broderick

Puzzle 6-20

You know the difference between you and me? I make this look good!

Will Smith

Puzzle 6-21

I'm gonna give you a little advice. There's a force in the universe that makes things happen, and all you have to do is get in touch with it. Stop thinking, let things happen, and be the ball.

Chevy Chase

Puzzle 6-22

The men may be the head of the house but the women are the neck and they can turn the head any way they want.

Lainie Kazan

Puzzle 6-23

Life is pain, Highness. Anyone who says differently is selling something.

Cary Elwes

Puzzle 6-24

Real loss is only possible when you love something more than you love yourself.

Robin Williams

Puzzle 6-25

We live and we die by time. And we must not commit the sin of losing our track on time.

Tom Hanks

Puzzle 6-26

Every night I cut out my heart. But in the morning it was full again.

Ralph Fiennes

Puzzle 6-27

Love? Above all things I believe in love. Love is like oxygen. Love is a many-splendored thing, love lifts us up where we belong, all you need is love.

Ewan McGregor

Puzzle 6-28

If I ever go looking for my heart's desire again, I won't look any further than my own back yard. Because if it isn't there, I never really lost it to begin with! Is that right?

Judy Garland

CHAPTER 7: IT'S ALL POLITICS

Puzzle 7-1

I know I have the body of a weak and feeble woman, but I have the heart and stomach of a King.

Queen Elizabeth I

Puzzle 7-2

We are not interested in the possibilities of defeat; they do not exist.

Queen Victoria

Puzzle 7-3

I was a queen, and you took away my crown; a wife, and you killed my husband; a mother, and you deprived me of my children. My blood alone remains: take it, but do not make me suffer long.

Marie Antoinette

Puzzle 7-4

Knavery seems to be so much the striking feature of its [America's] inhabitants that it may not in the end be an evil that they will become aliens to the kingdom.

King George III

Puzzle 7-5

You can't influence Europe's future from the terraces. You have to be on the pitch and playing hard.

John Major

Puzzle 7-6

The main essentials of a successful prime minister [are] sleep and a sense of history.

Harold Wilson

Puzzle 7-7

A leader must have the courage to act against an expert's advice.

James Callaghan

Puzzle 7-8

I will use all my strength to bring about a just society to a nation living in a tough world.

Pierre Elliott Trudeau

Puzzle 7-9

We should seek by all means in our power to avoid war, by analysing possible causes, by trying to remove them, by discussion in a spirit of collaboration and good will.

Neville Chamberlain

Puzzle 7-10

America is not anything if it consists of each of us. It is something only if it consists of all of us.

Woodrow Wilson

Puzzle 7-11

Sure, there are dishonest men in local government. But there are dishonest men in national government, too.

Richard Nixon

Puzzle 7-12

Every gun that is made, every warship launched, every rocket fired, signifies in a final sense a theft from those who hunger and are not fed, those who are cold and are not clothed.

Dwight D. Eisenhower

Puzzle 7-13

I have stepped out upon this platform that I may see you and that you may see me, and in the arrangement I have the best of the bargain.

Abraham Lincoln

Puzzle 7-14

I know I'm getting better at golf because I'm hitting fewer spectators.

Gerald Ford

Puzzle 7-15

I have often wanted to drown my troubles, but I can't get my wife to go swimming.

Jimmy Carter

Puzzle 7-16

I never drink coffee at lunch. I find it keeps me awake for the afternoon.

Ronald Reagan

Puzzle 7-17

Things are more like they are now than they ever were before.

Dwight D. Eisenhower

Puzzle 7-18

When we got into office, the thing that surprised me the most was that things were as bad as we'd been saying they were.

John F. Kennedy

Puzzle 7-19

It is easy to take liberty for granted, when you have never had it taken from you.

Dick Cheney

Puzzle 7-20

Bias and prejudice are attitudes to be kept in hand, not attitudes to be avoided.

Charles Curtis

Puzzle 7-21

American diplomacy is easy on the brain but hell on the feet.

Charles G. Dawes

Puzzle 7-22

For I would rather be a servant in the House of the Lord than to sit in the seats of the mighty.

Alben W. Barkley

Puzzle 7-23

Modern politics today requires a mastery of television. I've never really warmed up to television and, in fairness to television, it's never warmed up to me.

Walter F. Mondale

Puzzle 7-24

You must not fight too often with one enemy, or you will teach him all your art of war.

Napoleon Bonaparte

Puzzle 7-25

Politics is war without bloodshed, while war is politics with bloodshed.

Mao Tse-tung

Puzzle 7-26

A lie should be tried in a place where it will attract the attention of the world.

Ariel Sharon

Puzzle 7-27

One does not sell the earth upon which the people walk.

Crazy Horse

Puzzle 7-28

In politics it is necessary either to betray one's country or the electorate. I prefer to betray the electorate.

Charles De Gaulle

CHAPTER 8: RELIGION AND SPIRITUALITY

Puzzle 8-1

If God created us in his own image, we have more than reciprocated.

Voltaire

Puzzle 8-2

I believe in God like I believe in the sunrise. Not because I can see it, but because I can see all that it touches.

C. S. Lewis

Puzzle 8-3

I cannot conceive otherwise than that He, the Infinite Father, expects or requires no worship or praise from us, but that He is even infinitely above it.

Benjamin Franklin

Puzzle 8-4

Neither fire nor wind, birth nor death can erase our good deeds.

Puzzle 8-5

Your body is precious. It is our vehicle for awakening. Treat it with care.

Puzzle 8-6

An insincere and evil friend is more to be feared than a wild beast; a wild beast may wound your body, but an evil friend will wound your mind.

Puzzle 8-7

I hear and I forget. I see and I remember. I do and I understand.

Puzzle 8-8

Men's natures are alike, it is their habits that carry them far apart.

Puzzle 8-9

To see what is right, and not to do it, is want of courage or of principle.

Puzzle 8-10

He who speaks without modesty will find it difficult to make his words good.

Puzzle 8-11

When you know a thing, to hold that you know it; and when you do not know a thing, to allow that you do not know it—this is knowledge.

Puzzle 8-12

The ground on which we stand is sacred ground. It is the blood of our ancestors.

Chief Plenty Coups

Puzzle 8-13

The more you know, the more you will trust and the less you will fear.

Ojibway

Puzzle 8-14

These days people seek knowledge, not wisdom. Knowledge is of the past, wisdom is of the future.

Lumbee

Puzzle 8-15

May the warm winds of Heaven blow softly upon this home and the Great Spirit bless all who enter.

Cherokee Blessing

Puzzle 8-16

When you were born, you cried and the world rejoiced. Live your life so that when you die, the world cries and you rejoice.

White Elk

Puzzle 8-17

Be angry, and yet do not sin; do not let the sun go down on your anger.

Puzzle 8-18

Do unto others as you would have others do unto you.

Puzzle 8-19

And you will know the truth, and the truth will make you free.

Puzzle 8-20

Love is patient and kind; love is not jealous or boastful; it is not arrogant or rude.

Puzzle 8-21

We created man. We know the promptings of his soul, and are closer to him than the vein of his neck.

Puzzle 8-22

As for the unbelievers, their works are like a mirage in a desert.

Puzzle 8-23

He that chooses a religion over Islam, it will not be accepted from him and in the world to come he will be one of the lost.

Puzzle 8-24

Prophet, make war on the unbelievers and the hypocrites and deal rigorously with them. Hell shall be their home: an evil fate.

Puzzle 8-25

Beware of too much laughter, for it deadens the mind and produces oblivion.

Puzzle 8-26

Who can protest and does not, is an accomplice in the act.

Puzzle 8-27

A person will be called to account on Judgment Day for every permissible thing he might have enjoyed but did not.

Puzzle 8-28

Just as the soul fills the body, so God fills the world. Just as the soul bears the body, so God endures the world. Just as the soul sees but is not seen, so God sees but is not seen.

CHAPTER 9: SCIENTIFIC DISCOVERIES

Puzzle 9-1

A curious aspect of the theory of evolution is that everybody thinks he understands it.

Jacques Monod

Puzzle 9-2

However many ways there may be of being alive, it is certain that there are vastly more ways of being dead.

Richard Dawkins

Puzzle 9-3

Biology is the science of life in all its manifestations and is the key to all our futures.

David Bellamy

Puzzle 9-4

Every great advance in natural knowledge has involved the absolute rejection of authority.

Thomas Henry Huxley

Puzzle 9-5

Evolution, at least in the sense that Darwin speaks of it, cannot be detected within the lifetime of a single observer.

David B. Kitts

Puzzle 9-6

Chemistry is a trade for people without enough imagination to be physicists.

Arthur C. Clarke

Puzzle 9-7

One never notices what has been done; one can only see what remains to be done.

Marie Curie

Puzzle 9-8

If I have a thousand ideas and only one turns out to be good, I am satisfied.

Alfred Bernhard

Puzzle 9-9

As for butter versus margarine, I trust cows more than chemists.

Joan Gussow

Puzzle 9-10

No, this trick won't work . . . How on earth are you ever going to explain in terms of chemistry and physics so important a biological phenomenon as first love?

Albert Einstein

Puzzle 9-11

The digital revolution is far more significant than the invention of writing or even of printing.

Douglas Engelbart

Puzzle 9-12

I confess that I said to my brother Orville that man would not fly for fifty years.

Wilbur Wright

Puzzle 9-13

When one door closes another door opens; but we so often look so long and so regretfully upon the closed door, that we do not see the ones which open for us.

Alexander Graham Bell

Puzzle 9-14

Light makes photography. Embrace light. Admire it. Love it. But above all, know light. Know it for all you are worth, and you will know the key to photography.

George Eastman

Puzzle 9-15

A mathematician is a blind man in a dark room looking for a black cat which isn't there.

Charles Darwin

Puzzle 9-16

Nobody knows why, but the only theories which work are the mathematical ones.

Michael Holt

Puzzle 9-17

The mathematical sciences particularly exhibit order, symmetry, and limitation; and these are the greatest forms of the beautiful.

Aristotle

Puzzle 9-18

As far as the laws of mathematics refer to reality, they are not certain; and as far as they are certain, they do not refer to reality.

Albert Einstein

Puzzle 9-19

What is mind? No matter. What is matter? Never mind.

Thomas Hewitt Key

Puzzle 9-20

If you wish to make an apple pie truly from scratch, you must first invent the universe.

Carl Sagan

Puzzle 9-21

There are only two truly infinite things, the universe and stupidity. And I am unsure about the universe.

Albert Einstein

Puzzle 9-22

In physics, you don't have to go around making trouble for yourself—nature does it for you.

Frank Wilczek

Puzzle 9-23

One does not, by knowing all the physical laws as we know them today, immediately obtain an understanding of anything much.

Richard P. Feynman

Puzzle 9-24

That's the nature of research— you don't know what in hell you're doing.

Harold "Doc" Edgerton

Puzzle 9-25

Research is the act of going up alleys to see if they are blind.

Plutarch

Puzzle 9-26

If you steal from one author, it's plagiarism; if you steal from many, it's research.

Wilson Mizner

Puzzle 9-27

Basic research is what I'm doing when I don't know what I'm doing.

Wernher von Braun

Puzzle 9-28

The outcome of any serious research can only be to make two questions grow where only one grew before.

Thorstein Veblen

CHAPTER 10: PLAYING SPORTS

Puzzle 10-1

I have only one superstition. Touch all the bases when I hit a home run.

Babe Ruth

Puzzle 10-2

Whoever wants to know the heart and mind of America had better learn baseball.

Jacques Barzun

Puzzle 10-3

Baseball is the only field of endeavor where a man can succeed three times out of ten and be considered a good performer.

Ted Williams

Puzzle 10-4

Baseball is the favorite American sport because it's so slow. Any idiot can follow it. And just about any idiot can play it.

Gore Vidal

Puzzle 10-5

Sometimes a player's greatest challenge is coming to grips with his role on the team.

Scottie Pippen

Puzzle 10-6

Basketball is like photography: if you don't focus, all you have is the negative.

Dan Frisby

Puzzle 10-7

One man can be a crucial ingredient on a team, but one man cannot make a team.

Kareem Abdul-Jabbar

Puzzle 10-8

When I dunk, I put something on it. I want the ball to hit the floor before I do.

Darryl Dawkins

Puzzle 10-9

Basketball is like war in that offensive weapons are developed first, and it always takes a while for the defense to catch up.

Red Auerbach

Puzzle 10-10

Football features two of the worst aspects of American life, violence and committee meetings.

George Will

Puzzle 10-11

The way you motivate a football team is to eliminate the unmotivated ones.

Lou Holtz

Puzzle 10-12

You have to play this game like somebody just hit your mother with a two-by-four.

Dan Birdwell

Puzzle 10-13

Football isn't a contact sport, it's a collision sport. Dancing is a contact sport.

Duffy Daugherty

Puzzle 10-14

Some people think football is a matter of life and death. I don't like that attitude. I can assure them it is much more serious than that.

Bill Shankly

Puzzle 10-15

Golf is the most fun you can have without taking your clothes off.

Chi Chi Rodriguez

Puzzle 10-16

If you think it's hard to meet new people, try picking up the wrong golf ball.

Jack Lemmon

Puzzle 10-17

If you are going to throw a club, it is important to throw it ahead

of you, down the fairway, so you don't waste energy going back to pick it up.

Tommy Bolt

Puzzle 10-18
Golf appeals to the idiot in us and the child. Just how childlike golf players become is proven by their frequent inability to count past five.

John Updike

Puzzle 10-19
One hundred percent of the shots you don't take don't go in.

Wayne Gretzky

Puzzle 10-20
Ice hockey is a form of disorderly conduct in which the score is kept.

Doug Larson

Puzzle 10-21
I went to a fight the other night and a hockey game broke out.

Rodney Dangerfield

Puzzle 10-22
All hockey players are bilingual. They know English and profanity.

Gordie Howe

Puzzle 10-23
Hockey's a funny game. You have to prove yourself every shift, every game. It's not up to anybody else. You have to take pride in yourself.

Paul Coffey

Puzzle 10-24
From what we get, we can make a living; what we give, however, makes a life.

Arthur Ashe

Puzzle 10-25
Writing free verse is like playing tennis with the net down.

Robert Frost

Puzzle 10-26
If someone says tennis is not feminine, I say screw it.

Rosie Casals

Puzzle 10-27
Tennis is an addiction that once it has truly hooked a man will not let him go.

Russell Lynes

Puzzle 10-28
Tennis belongs to the individual- istic past—a hero, or at most a

pair of friends or lovers, against the world.

> Jacques Barzun

CHAPTER 11: CRYPTOGRAM JUMBLE

Puzzle 11-1

Success is not the result of spontaneous combustion. You must set yourself on fire.

> Reggie Leach

Puzzle 11-2

Our scientific power has outrun our spiritual power. We have guided missiles and misguided men.

> Martin Luther King, Jr.

Puzzle 11-3

I disapprove of what you say, but will defend to the death your right to say it.

> Voltaire

Puzzle 11-4

What you are is God's gift to you. What you make of yourself is your gift back to God.

> Kelly Jeppesen

Puzzle 11-5

Because only if you've been in the deepest valley can you ever know how magnificent it is to be on the highest mountain.

> Richard M. Nixon

Puzzle 11-6

Tenderness and kindness are not signs of weakness and despair, but manifestations of strength and resolution.

> Kahlil Gibran

Puzzle 11-7

It's amazing that the amount of news that happens in the world every day always just exactly fits the newspaper.

> Jerry Seinfeld

Puzzle 11-8

There are two lasting bequests we can give our children. One is roots. The other is wings.

> Hodding Carter, Jr.

Puzzle 11-9

Forgive, O Lord, my little jokes on Thee, and I'll forgive Thy great big joke on me.

> Robert Frost

Puzzle 11-10

I may not have gone where I intended to go, but I think I have ended up where I intended to be.

Douglas Adams

Puzzle 11-11

Money and success don't change people; they merely amplify what is already there.

Will Smith

Puzzle 11-12

You're never as good as everyone tells you when you win, and you're never as bad as they say when you lose.

Lou Holtz

Puzzle 11-13

Don't worry about people stealing your ideas. If your ideas are any good, you'll have to ram them down people's throats.

Howard Aiken

Puzzle 11-14

I always turn to the sports pages first, which records people's accomplishments. The front page has nothing but man's failures.

Chief Justice Earl Warren

Puzzle 11-15

Progress always involves risk; you can't steal second base and keep your foot on first base.

Frederick Wilcox

Puzzle 11-16

When I'm inspired, I get excited because I can't wait to see what I'll come up with next.

Dolly Parton

Puzzle 11-17

Courage is doing what you are afraid to do. There can be no courage unless you're scared.

Eddie Rickenbacher

Puzzle 11-18

Supreme excellence consists in breaking the enemy's resistance without fighting.

Sun-Tzu

Puzzle 11-19

The trouble with having an open mind, of course, is that people will insist on coming along and trying to put things in it.

Terry Pratchett

Puzzle 11-20

The man who does not work for the love of work but only

for money is not likely to make money nor find much fun in life.
Charles Schwab

Puzzle 11-21
Computers make it easier to do a lot of things, but most of the things they make it easier to do don't need to be done.
Andy Rooney

Puzzle 11-22
Be bold. If you're going to make an error, make a doozy, and don't be afraid to hit the ball.
Billie Jean King

Puzzle 11-23
Every artist dips his brush in his own soul, and paints his own nature into his pictures.
Henry Ward Beecher